England in the 17th Century: The History of E
the Glorious Revolut

By Charles River Editors

A depiction of William of Orange boarding a ship for England

About Charles River Editors

Charles River Editors is a boutique digital publishing company, specializing in bringing history back to life with educational and engaging books on a wide range of topics. Keep up to date with our new and free offerings with this 5 second sign up on our weekly mailing list, and visit Our Kindle Author Page to see other recently published Kindle titles.

We make these books for you and always want to know our readers' opinions, so we encourage you to leave reviews and look forward to publishing new and exciting titles each week.

Introduction

A 1656 portrait of Oliver Cromwell

England in the 17th Century

"We have great reason to believe, we shall be every day in a worse condition than we are, and less able to defend ourselves, and therefore we do earnestly wish we might be so happy as to find a remedy before it be too late for us to contribute to our own deliverance ... the people are so generally dissatisfied with the present conduct of the government, in relation to their religion, liberties and properties (all which have been greatly invaded), and they are in such expectation of their prospects being daily worse, that your Highness may be assured, there are nineteen parts of twenty of the people throughout the kingdom, who are desirous of a change; and who, we believe, would willingly contribute to it, if they had such a protection to countenance their rising, as would secure them from being destroyed. – Excerpt from the invitation by The Seven to William of Orange to become monarch

17th century Europe, particularly its latter years, is often hailed as the beginning of the Enlightenment as nations across the continent experienced a surge in innovation and scientific progress, a period also commonly referred to as the Age of Reason. There was English natural philosopher, Francis Bacon, whose book *Novum Organum* challenged Aristotelian philosophy and stressed the significance of inductive reasoning. Bacon's ideas, which emphasized observation and the implementation of various premises to form conclusions, was later referenced by famed French mathematician René Descartes.

Bacon

This illustrious age also inspired a brilliant burst in art and creativity. Progressive but hot button topics were greeted with resounding choruses of approval. One of these forward-thinkers was renowned English philosopher, John Locke, one of the forefathers of political liberalism. Locke was a staunch believer in the abolishment of the Divine Right of Kings, which was the God-given right for monarchs to rule over a nation. This was an archaic system wherein rebellion was considered the worst of all political crimes, and a system that not only made tyranny much more probable but condoned it. Locke was opposed to the doctrine of papal infallibility, which essentially rendered the pope faultless when it came to his teachings about religion and morals, though this has since been disputed by the modern Catholic Church. This was one of the driving points of his opposition towards an English Catholic king. Locke, a follower of Thomas Hobbes, another respected player in the field, echoed the idea that men are intrinsically free and independent souls, born with no obligation or duty to one another, and should be able to pursue whatever interest they so pleased.

Locke

These radical ideas were bordering on blasphemous, but it was, perhaps, in a sense, necessary. The Enlightenment had been awakened by the European Age of Discovery, a transformative era that succeeded the Medieval Years of Yore, but the continent was also a seedbed of insurrection, holy wars, and volatility. People were growing weary of the unpredictable system of monarchy, a post that was inherited only by members of an exclusive bloodline or connection, one that often muted the voices of the people.

Time and time again, grossly incompetent and seemingly diabolic rulers had come to power through the rigged regal system. For starters, there was John, King of England, the real-life inspiration of the evil and infantile lion in the beloved Disney animation *Robin Hood*, a retelling of the tale with anthropomorphic animals. King John was said to have been power-hungry but politically feckless, and a sadistic soul who delighted in cruel and inhumane torture. The king did away with nearly everyone that had slighted him, including his own nephew, his political rival. This was a man whose reputation was so horrid, chroniclers and academics have summed him up as an "absolute rotter."

Then, there was Queen Mary I of England, who earned herself the less-than-pleasant moniker of "Bloody Mary." While in power, Mary vowed to restore papal authority and revert England to Catholicism, placing the bullseye on Protestants. Laws against heresy made a bloody comeback, which saw hundreds of Protestants dragged to the stakes. Naturally, the oppressed began to revolt. Bands of insurgents flooded the city streets, torching city buildings and governmental establishments. Ambitious assassination plots were hatched across the land as conspirators conjured up planned poisonings, midnight sneak attacks, and other desperate ways to dispose of the tyrants.

The same religious strife led to one of England's most notorious assassination attempts. In 1605, Guy Fawkes was one of over a dozen conspirators in the famous Gunpowder Plot, an attempt to assassinate England's King James I. When the plot was discovered on the 5th of November, Fawkes and other conspirators were quickly convicted and executed, and the King asked his subjects to remember the date as "the joyful day of deliverance." Fawkes was but one of a countless number of failed assassins, but in a perversely ironic way, the king's declaration ultimately turned November 5 into Guy Fawkes Day, a celebratory day that usually had children creating an effigy that would then be burned in a bonfire. While the effigy was usually Fawkes, others made it a custom to burn an effigy of the pope, a tradition that came to the 13 Colonies in America as well. Though he was only one of the plotters, Fawkes became the one most associated with the act, and he was viewed as a symbol of treason.

King James I would continue to reign, and England has more often been faced with the claims of competing kings and queens than with a period of no monarch at all. The major exception to that rule came in the 11 years between 1649 and 1660, when England was a republic. Following the disastrous reign of Charles I and the civil wars that led to his execution, Parliament and the army ruled England. England's republican experiment started out as a work of collaboration and compromise; lords, army officers and members of Parliament (MPs) worked together to find a political settlement that did not include the despised royal House of Stuart. Nonetheless, religious and political division made collective rule unworkable, and ultimately, one man emerged from the chaos to rule the country. He had risen from a humble background to become the leading general of the Civil Wars, and as a man of staunch beliefs and ruthless pragmatism, he controlled England from 1653-1658 under the title of Lord Protector. In essence, he was a king in all but name.

That man was Oliver Cromwell, and in the popular imagination, Cromwell has overshadowed the rest of the leaders of the parliamentary cause and the New Model Army. His name is known by everyone in England, while parliamentary leaders like John Pym, constitutional reformers like John Lambert, and even Sir Thomas Fairfax, who led Parliament's army through most of the wars, are known only to history buffs. But Cromwell has also been one of the most controversial figures in English history ever since. Viewed by some as a despot and others as a champion of liberty, Cromwell's legacy is so diverse that while many Irish accuse him of genocide, others look at him as a social revolutionary.

Cromwell's death would lead to a restoration of the royal line, but an uprising of a completely different nature would soon unfold on English soil – the Glorious Revolution, an intriguing story of a power war exacerbated by ruthless ambition, under-the-table plotting, and the treachery of familial betrayal. In 1678, a sinister scheme to assassinate King Charles II was unearthed, sending the public into a frenzy of mass panic. Fingers were pointed at the Catholics, who had been accused of concocting the elaborate conspiracy, and this very event would intensify the white-hot flames of the Anti-Catholic hysteria that was already running unchecked within the nation. 7 years later, the openly Catholic King James II rose to the throne, and needless to say, the largely Protestant public was anything but pleased. As the people slowly turned against him, the king's daughter, Mary, and her husband, William of Orange, watched across the English Channel from a distance. The people were begging for change in a broken system, and something drastic had to and would be done.

England in the 17th Century: The History of England from King James I to the Glorious Revolution examines some of the most tumultuous periods in England's history. Along with pictures depicting important people, places, and events, you will learn about 17th century England like never before.

England in the 17th Century: The History of England from King James I to the Glorious Revolution

About Charles River Editors

Introduction

    The Tudors and King James I

    Oliver Cromwell and the Road to War

    The Civil Wars

    The Commonwealth and the Lord Protector

    The Restoration

    King James II and William of Orange

    Broken Promises

    Rumors, Conspiracy, and the Final Straw

    The Glorious Revolution

    Online Resources

    Bibliography

Free Books by Charles River Editors

Discounted Books by Charles River Editors

The Tudors and King James I

"Monarchy is the greatest thing on earth. Kings are rightly called gods since just like God they have the power of life and death over all their subjects in all things...so it is a crime for anyone to argue about what a king can do." – King James I

The tale of Bloody Mary is a chilling phenomenon that has become a common element in Halloween and Western sleepover traditions. Legend has it that her ghostly figure can be summoned in the bathroom of one's very own home. For generations, fearless children have put this game to the test. First, the child locks the bathroom door and switches off all the lights. Cloaked in darkness, they then light a single candle and take their position before a mirror, chanting her name 3 times in a row. Once Bloody Mary is summoned, the child is greeted by a benevolent, but sad spirit that blinks back at them before once again retreating into nothingness. Others, however, have reported that an unfortunate few who have angered the spirit left the bathroom with their eyes clawed out and their limbs covered in raw scratch marks. Some would disappear behind the mirror for the rest of eternity.

What many people don't realize is that the urban legend of Bloody Mary was inspired by none other than Queen Mary I of England. Once she had taken the throne, she vowed to demolish the nation's Anglican ways and bring her people back to Roman Catholicism. Only, those who dared challenge her ways were met with a slow and fiery demise at the stake. Her 5-year rule may have been short-lived, but her persecution of 284 Protestant heretics was ultimately what led to the birth of her nickname.

Bloody Mary

In fact, Mary I was just one name in the long line of Tudors, a Welsh-English family that ruled England and Wales for over a century. As tyrannous as her methods may have been, it does not compare to the barbarism inflicted upon the people during her father's reign. Her father, King Henry VIII, was responsible for an estimated 57,000-72,000 deaths in his 37 years of power. To put that into perspective, that comes to roughly 1,946 kingdom-sanctioned deaths a year, and making matters worse, those who were not beheaded were faced with a slew of medieval torture tactics that would make death most welcome. According to historian, L.A. Parry, the use of torture "reached its height" during the Tudors' reign. Those who refused the king's ways were subjected to solitary confinement, seemingly endless interrogation tactics, and inflicted with debilitating physical pain. Some prisoners were caged in tiny little cells called the "Little Ease," where they could neither lay down or stand upright. Some were manacled by the wrists and dangled off the ground for hours or days on end. Some were sprawled out on a rack, their limbs stretched further apart with a crank of a lever. Others found themselves on the "Scavenger's Daughter," a humiliating device used to hold prisoners in a fetal position, compressing them until their bones, ribs, and organs were crushed. There were dozens who were thrown into vats of boiling oil, tar, or lead, where they were literally fried alive. The list of horrors went on and on.

Henry VIII

Henry VIII's reign of terror began when he became dissatisfied with his wife, Catherine of Aragon, for her failure to bear a son for him. The king called for a divorce, but became infuriated when his request was promptly denied by the Roman Catholic Church. Taking matters into his own hands, he then decided to form the Anglican Church and dubbed himself the "supreme head" of the Church of England through the Act of Supremacy of 1534. 4 years later, Pope Paul III declared that the king was to be excommunicated from the Catholic Church.

Armed with his new self-given title, Henry VIII was motivated to bring the Protestant Reformation to his kingdom. Even as he technically insisted that some trappings of Catholicism remain in practice, across the nation, monasteries were scrapped and Roman Catholic churches were pulverized to enrich the kingdom. His majesty also ordered the first authorized English edition of the Christian Bible ("the Great Bible") to be put in every single parish in England. By 1541, 9,000 copies of the Great Bible had been produced and distributed across the country.

The tens of thousands that perished under his iron fist were not just limited to heretics and naysayers of his new church. Among those executed included potential rivals to his throne, as well as leaders of the Pilgrimage of Grace. Family and friends were not spared – along with Thomas Cromwell, the king's own trusted advisor, 2 of his wives and their supposed lovers were also sent to their gruesome deaths. If anything, Henry VIII remains England's most well-known monarch because of such executions.

After Henry's death and the premature death of his teenaged son Edward, his daughter Mary took the throne. The daughter of Catherine of Aragon, the devoutly Catholic Queen Mary I did everything in her power to dissociate herself from everything her father stood for, but her mission to reunite England with the Catholic Church did not go far. When Mary I died in 1558 at the age of 42, possibly from ovarian cancer, her half-sister Elizabeth, the daughter of Henry VIII and Anne Boleyn, took her place.

Elizabeth I

Because Queen Elizabeth I was considered an unlikely and illegitimate heir to the throne, her rule was met with frequent interruptions of rebellion and turmoil, but the 25-year-old queen was set on making a name for herself. She proudly declared herself a bachelorette, the "Virgin Queen," choosing to forgo a romantic marriage, as she saw it as a potential threat to her throne. Instead, she dedicated her life to her kingdom and her people alone.

In the early years of her reign, the Protestant-raised queen decided to tread lightly. Aware that many of the noble men who held some of the top positions in the government were of Catholic faith, Elizabeth I decided it would be best to keep an open mind. Though public services were still prohibited, as long as Catholics could prove their loyalty to the queen, they would be left to pray freely behind closed doors.

Still, many were less than pleased with the queen's seemingly hazy stance on Catholicism in England. It appeared that only influential Catholics mattered to the queen. The Catholic commoners, on the other hand, were outright discriminated against. Not long after, the people began to rebel, and the queen found herself the prime target of one attempted assassination after another. In 1569, the Revolt of the Earls became one of the first to challenge her authority. The failed uprising was led by the Earls of Northumberland and Westmoreland, a pair of Catholics that had sworn loyalty to the queen. Elizabeth I took great offense to this, concluding that Catholics were, as she had suspected, conniving and untrustworthy. In her eyes, they had spit right in her face when she had been so "tolerant" of them up until now.

The straw that would break the camel's back came a year later, when Pope Pius V announced a Papal Bull of excommunication against the queen. The pope lambasted Elizabeth I as a "usurper of the throne," with phrases such as "heretic" and "wicked" peppered into his speech. And much to the queen's alarm, the pope encouraged Catholics to "deprive" her of her throne, and even went so far as to declare it a sinless act of great honor.

With that, whatever tolerance Elizabeth I had for the Catholics vanished, and when more and more Jesuits trickled into her kingdom on a mission to further spread their Catholic faith, the queen decided that something had to be done. William Cecil, the queen's chief advisor, recommended that Catholic heretics and those who refused to pay allegiance to the kingdom be immediately executed, and that was exactly what the queen did. By 1585, an Act of Parliament was issued to banish all the Jesuits and Catholics from the kingdom for good. Furthermore, Catholicism in England was now equivalent to an act of treason. 3 decades ago, many Catholics found peace in simply performing masses in the privacy of their own homes. Now, not only was that right stripped from them, it was as if they had red rings painted on the back of their heads.

The most devout Catholics were undeterred by Elizabeth I's attempts at squashing their faith. In order to avoid hefty fines and prison time, they began to improvise more ways to avoid the probing eyes of the kingdom spies. As Catholic priests were now rendered illegal, Catholics carried around miniature mass kits and portable alter stones stuffed in their pockets. They had to be especially sneaky with personal prayer items such as rosary beads, as they were deemed "superstitious" paraphernalia by the kingdom. Anyone caught with prayer beads faced the risk of having their lands and goods seized.

Catholics scattered around the kingdom showed their defiance whenever they could. Many kept journals of their small acts of rebellion. One man by the name of Sir Richard Shireburn attended Protestant services with wool lodged in his ears for 2 years straight. Many reportedly refused Protestant communion and would slip the wafers up their sleeves to chuck in the trash after service.

The queen quickly caught wind of those who were playing hooky. When she realized inputting a fine of 12 pence (**£12.93 purchasing power today**) for missing church was not enough to fill the pews, the price was jacked up to 20 pounds (**£5,174**) in 1581. Yet even with the crippling fines and lawful confinement looming over their heads, an estimated 8,590 of the estimated 40,000 were branded "disobedient" in 1603.

Towards the end of the queen's reign, her aggression against Catholics only intensified. Catholic priests who were caught conducting mass behind her back were severely tortured, publicly humiliated, and slain. One of them was Edmund Campion, a priest who had managed to charm the queen upon a visit to Oxford in 1566. When he was caught, Elizabeth I had him tortured and hung at Tyburn. Many reported to have seen the empty bloody beds of his fingernails as he hung limply from his noose. Robert Southwell, a Jesuit and famed poet, had his head sliced clean off his neck. His rotting head was then displayed for the crowds to see, attracting flies, rotten vegetables, curses, and the cries of "traitor" from passersby.

Campion

Perhaps one of the most well-known among Elizabeth I's lengthy casualty list was the Catholic-born Mary Stuart, best known as Mary, Queen of Scots. Mary's was an unusual reign in a tumultuous period, and her tragedy was intertwined with her country's transformation. In Mary's case, she was a second cousin once removed of England's Queen Elizabeth I, which made her a rival for the throne; Mary was the granddaughter of Margaret Tudor, Henry VIII's sister, and her Catholicism made Mary the true and rightful Queen of England in the eyes of many Catholics and the Vatican.

Mary, Queen of Scots

These facts, coupled with the realization that several English Catholics (especially rebels active in the Rising of the North movement) supported Mary, understandably made Elizabeth I uneasy. Mary also did not help herself when she married James Hepburn, 4th Earl of Bothwell, who was widely accused of raping her. The Scottish people rebelled, and Mary abdicated and fled southwards towards England.

Elizabeth I was unsure at first what to do with Mary, so she kept Mary imprisoned in several castles and manor houses inside England (making escape difficult and thus unlikely). After 18 years and 9 months in Elizabeth's custody, it became clear that the situation was becoming untenable, mainly due to Catholic efforts on the continent and within England to have Elizabeth I assassinated and to raise Mary to England's throne after marrying her to the recusant Catholic Thomas Howard, Duke of Norfolk.

By some accounts, Elizabeth's spymaster and principal secretary Francis Walsingham, either trapped Mary or fabricated evidence on high treason charges associated with the plot initiated by

Anthony Babington. In 1587, Mary was executed for her involvement in conspiracies to assassinate Elizabeth, and everything involving her execution was burned in the aftermath so that there would be no souvenirs would be left for relic hunters, and there would be no bloody clothes that might become a symbol of Mary as a Catholic martyr. All the while, Elizabeth is said to have had deep misgivings about executing a fellow sovereign and thereby setting a pernicious precedent, nor could Elizabeth forget that her own mother, Anne Boleyn (though only a queen consort), had also been executed.

By the end of Elizabeth I's 45-year reign, a documented 30 people were executed after the Papal Bull. Other sources would suggest the number of Catholic martyrs that lost their lives could have been as high as 300. Putting aside her aggression towards the Catholics, many still credit the queen with leaving the nation at a Golden Age at the time of her death. Because of the many successful voyages of discovery and the flourishing of the arts during her reign, Elizabeth I is often hailed as one of the greatest monarchs to have ever ruled England.

However, even though she had put Mary to death, Elizabeth's unmarried and childless status left no Tudor to follow her. Thus, she was succeeded by Mary's son James, whose reign united the two kingdoms of England and Scotland. When King James I succeeded the throne in 1603, there was an aura of hope among the people. He was tall, broad-shouldered, with sunken but wise eyes, wavy brown hair, a well-groomed light beard, and a prominent bulbous-tipped nose. The fact that his mother was Catholic, coupled with his background experience as the King of Scotland, gave the Catholics of England new reason to believe that change was coming. With the death of Elizabeth I concluding the reign of the Tudors, Catholics were hopeful that a new era of acceptance and religious freedom would soon fall in place. Unfortunately, this would prove to be far from the case.

King James I

In the heady early days of his reign, King James I was viewed as undoubtedly one of the most intelligent and academically versed of all the English and Scottish royals. In addition to authorizing the King James Version of the Bible, which remains one of the most popular books in production to date, he penned several books himself. And as the first to hold the title for King of England, Scotland, and France at the same time, his power skyrocketed.

Like his mother's cousin, James I hoped to begin his reign by showing tolerance of the Catholics; after all, his mother had been Catholic and his own wife had converted to Catholicism not too long ago. However, as it quickly became clear to him that England was overwhelmingly populated with anti-Catholic Protestants, he knew that he had no choice but to comply with the majority. Thus, the king announced a separation from the church and state, which eliminated the power of the Pope and the Roman Catholic Church among his people. From there, he continued the persecutions of English Catholics and imposed even heavier fines and penalties on those who disobeyed him.

Naturally, the Catholics' resentment for the kingdom intensified, especially because just a few months before the death of the queen, a man named Everard Digby reportedly made 3 separate treks to Scotland and secretly met with the king. Digby promised James I the support of the Catholics if he promised to lift all the bans imposed by Elizabeth I. When James I agreed, Digby returned home, spreading the good news to the Catholic community. Needless to say, when the king went back on his word, Catholics all around England felt as if they had been stiffed.

Digby

Robert Cecil, the chief advisor of Queen Elizabeth I at the time of her demise, kept his position and now directly reported to James I. A devout Protestant himself, he took every opportunity to remind the king that all Catholics were "traitors," adamant that their allegiance was to Rome and not to the kingdom. Like the previous monarch, James I took this to heart.

Another interesting facet that some historians believed to have contributed to the king's animosity towards the Catholic Church was his alleged bisexuality. Though Anne of Denmark bore 8 of his children, there have been multiple accounts of the king's romantic relationships with men before and during his reign. One of these accounts spoke of an incident in the 1580s, when the king openly kissed an earl in full view of the public.

Shortly after ascending to the throne in 1603, King James went even further than Catholics' worst nightmares and ordered all Catholic priests to leave England. The betrayal, or at least what Catholics saw as a betrayal, was complete.

This act so annoyed some Catholics, including Guy Fawkes, that they decided to kill James by blowing up the Houses of Parliament when James came to open Parliament. The intention was to replace him on the throne with his Catholic daughter, Elizabeth of Scotland.[1] James and his daughter were hardly the only family divided by religion, as intra-familial blood feuds had begun with King Henry VIII's Protestant Reformation and the Dissolution of the Monasteries. Brother turned against brother, sister against sister, and here daughter against father. What was even more interesting is that the alleged pretender did not even need to be opposed by the alternative; what Elizabeth of Scotland wanted for her father was irrelevant, as others with vested interest took it upon themselves. It did happen sometimes, as with Lade Jane Grey's execution by Bloody Mary, that one of the parties lost their life for no fault or even action of their own.

---

[1] The irony of ironies is that it is through Elizabeth that the Protestant Hanoverians would come to rule England after Queen Anne's dynasts would all die out.

Elizabeth of Scotland

Catholic plots against James I had been foiled in 1603 shortly after he took the throne, including the Main Plot, which had the support and participation of Sir Walter Raleigh. The Bye Plot, which was hatched up by Catholic priests planning to kidnap the King, was revealed by fellow Catholics. the priests William Watson and William Clark planned to kidnap James and hold him in the Tower of London until he agreed to be more tolerant towards Catholics.

Of course, none of those are anywhere near as notorious as the Gunpowder Plot, in which Fawkes and his accomplices plotted to kill James and everyone sitting in the Houses of Parliament when James opened Parliament on 5 November 1605.

Guy Fawkes and his fellow conspirators, having rented out a house right by the Houses of Parliament, managed to smuggle 36 barrels of gunpowder into a cellar of the House of Lords.

The other conspirators were Robert and Thomas Wintour, Thomas Percy, Christopher and John Wright, Francis Tresham, Everard Digby, Ambrose Rookwood, Thomas Bates, Robert Keyes, Hugh Owen, John Grant and Robert Catesby. Though his name is all but lost to history, it was Robert Catesby who was the mastermind of the plot, while it was Fawkes who had learned the art of explosives. It was merely Fawkes' responsibility to set off the fuse, which is why he was the one who was initially caught and remembered when the plot was unfoiled.

Oliver Cromwell and the Road to War

Born on April 25, 1599 in Huntingdon, Oliver Cromwell was the son of Robert Cromwell and Elizabeth Steward, and despite being the fifth of 10 children, he was the only boy in the family to survive infancy in an era when child mortality was still quite high. The Cromwell's were descended from a sister of Thomas Cromwell (c.1485-1540), a famous minister for King Henry VIII. The family had become wealthy during the Reformation when they took over property confiscated by Henry VIII from the church, and though they switched between the surnames of Williams and Cromwell, by the 1590s they were well settled within the landed gentry of Huntingdonshire in the English East Midlands.

Portrait of Thomas Cromwell

Oliver's grandfather, Sir Henry Williams, was the second richest landowner in the county, but while he had many children, Robert was one of the younger ones, so he inherited only a small portion of land and a house in Huntingdon. This left the Cromwell's still part of the landed gentry but in its lower tier, with an income from the land of up to £300 per year.

England at the time was a very hierarchical country. Someone of Oliver's birth could be expected to live comfortably but never to make a huge name for himself. As Cromwell himself later put it, he was destined to live 'neither in considerable height, nor yet in obscurity'. This was a time in England's history when political, social and economic leadership were almost entirely dictated by birth. An aristocrat might rise from the lower ranks of the nobility to the upper ones, or go down the other way. A small merchant might become moderately wealthy, but most people never left the station in which they were born, and for the vast majority this meant a life as a peasant farmer, working the land, attending church on Sunday, and seldom traveling more than a dozen miles from home.

However, while the lives of ordinary people remained stable and unchanging, people of power and influence were trying to maintain power in tumultuous times. The growth in artistic and intellectual endeavour unleashed by the Renaissance meant that ideas were growing and changing faster than at any point in history. The 16th century had then seen the rise of the Protestant Reformation across the continent, and in some regions, including England, Protestants had gone from oppressed heretics to the dominant religious group, while the Catholic Church and its supporters eagerly fought back. A growth in international exploration and trade was also causing economic upheaval. Inevitably these changes created conflicts, conflicts which sometimes spiraled into violence and even war, and though no one could have predicted it at his birth, these changes would come to define Oliver Cromwell's life and legacy.

Like the vast majority of people in England at the time, the Cromwell's were Christian, and Oliver was christened four days after his birth. Even in England, separated by sea from its neighbors, religious reform and controversy were in the air. The Protestant reform movement was shaking Europe, with theologians following the teachings of Calvin and Luther and preaching a radical reformation of the church, away from the old Catholic hierarchies and towards a new approach in which each Christian had access to God's word through translations of the Bible. In England, this was accompanied by King Henry VIII's break from the authority of the Pope, setting up a separate Church of England, but this was a church founded on political rather than doctrinal ideology, and while some preachers were trying to push it towards the Protestant extreme of Puritanism, others favored a far more elaborate Catholic-style religion referred to as Arminianism. England's religious divisions were awkward ones, and for that reason the monarch and their advisers often avoided tackling them. At the same time, however, this meant the divisions were allowed to grow.

From around 1604, Oliver attended Huntingdon Grammar School, where he was taught by Puritan scholar Thomas Beard. Beard became a friend of the family and a big influence on Oliver, and his presence in the young man's life is indicative both of the family's religious leanings and of the direction Oliver's faith would eventually take him in. He was growing up in a tradition which challenged authority, even while enforcing a strict moral code that was quick to preach the word of righteousness and condemn its opponents.

After Huntingdon, Cromwell went up to Cambridge, where he studied at Sidney Sussex College. The college had been founded in 1596 using funds left in the will of Frances Sidney, Countess of Sussex, and it was from the start a firmly Protestant institution with a Puritan ethos. However, Cromwell never completed his studies at Cambridge, leaving in 1617 to look after his mother and seven unmarried sisters following the death of his father. From there, he may have received training at Lincoln's Inn in London, one of several legal inns responsible for training England's legal minds for a place in court, but while several of his ancestors had trained there and his son would also do so, no record of Oliver's presence remains at the Inn.

On August 22, 1620 Cromwell married Elizabeth Bourchier, the daughter of a leather merchant and Essex land owner. Over the next 18 years, the couple had nine children: five boys and four girls. Of the boys, one died in infancy and two in early adulthood, and it was the third son, Richard, who would eventually become Cromwell's heir.

Portrait of Cromwell's wife

Portrait of Richard Cromwell

Marriage brought Cromwell into the same social circles as many of London's leading merchants. This was an influential network of successful businessmen, influenced by the political schemes of the Earls of Holland and Warwick. London was the economic and political heart of England, and it held huge influence over the country and its government. The London mob had been known to proclaim kings and lynch politicians, while the city's merchants and craftsmen connected England into the growing global economy. To be a man of influence in London was to be a man of influence on the stage of England.

Still, not everything went smoothly for Cromwell. By 1628, he was suffering from would now be considered depression, which at its worst made daily activities almost unbearable. Still a relatively minor local figure, Cromwell also found himself caught up in a dispute among Huntingdon's gentry about a new charter for the town, and he had to appear before the royal Privy Council as a result. It was probably because of this that he sold most of his Huntingdon property and moved to St. Ives in Cambridgeshire.

Now reduced to the social and economic status of yeoman farmers, Cromwell and his brother Henry kept a smallholding on which they raised sheep and chickens, but in 1636, his fortunes took another turn when he inherited not only various property in Ely but the job of tithe collector for Ely Cathedral from a maternal uncle. Such inherited jobs were common at the time, and some could provide a living for relatively little work. This brought his income back up to its previous level, if not higher, and returned him to the ranks of the gentry.

Cromwell's house in Ely

Cromwell's personal and financial crises of the 1620s and 1630s also brought about a religious transformation in him. Though always Protestant, he had not always been a Puritan, and as late as 1626, he showed signs of a less radical faith, despite his education and family influences. However, in the 1630s, he experienced a religious awakening, coming around to the Puritan perspective of the religious independents. He believed that the Reformation had not gone far enough, that England remained a sinful place, and that Catholic ideas and practices needed to be completely excised from the church. This was about more than the moderate Protestantism espoused by the English bishops; it was about tearing up centuries of tradition and starting afresh.

Thanks to the patronage of powerful friends, Cromwell became a Member of Parliament (MP) in the last three Parliaments of King Charles I's reign. He was not a major player in the political maneuvers that eventually led to war, but to understand what followed, it is necessary to understand what happened, and how a new and relatively unimportant MP like Cromwell could fit into the picture.

King Charles I

The relationship between the English monarch and Parliament was an ever-shifting one, as there was no written constitution setting out their relative powers but instead a series of compromises and precedents. Originally a way for the king to gather influential people together, listen to their advice, and persuade them to support his policies, Parliament had turned into an institution with its own distinctive role and traditions. By the early 17th century, it was growing in both significance and confidence, and many MPs believed that they had not just a right but a duty to curb the excesses of the monarch. King Charles I, on the other hand, believed that he was appointed by God and had the right to rule without restriction, even if he found himself unable to do so without Parliament's cooperation.

When Charles inherited the throne in 1625, he was received with suspicion in Parliament. The MPs and Lords who made up the two houses of Parliament were, like the rest of the country, predominantly Protestant, with a growing and vocal Puritan minority. Charles on the other hand was a high church Arminian, who within months of becoming king married Catholic French princess Henrietta Maria at a time when the French king was suppressing Protestants. His favorite advisers included the Arminian Bishop William Laud, who wanted to enforce Catholic-style practices within the church. To an English gentry who saw Catholicism as a foreign threat, this king's agenda was extremely suspect, and his lavish lifestyle appalled the Puritans.

William Laud

The other great source of political division involved the royal finances. Much like the rules of the English church and Parliament, those around taxation had been laid down in confusing and contradictory ways over time rather than clearly set out and agreed upon. Needing money to fund foreign wars, but unable to get the taxes he wanted through Parliament, Charles used forced loans and manipulated precedents to raise funds. This angered the people he was taking money from, as well as many MPs, who found themselves deprived of the political leverage that came with granting taxes.

Things started to come to a head in March 1629 when Parliament refused to provide the king with the taxes he wanted. He closed down Parliament, as was his right, but not before MPs had made resolutions against Catholicism, Arminianism and Charles's schemes to raise money. Nine MPs were arrested on the King's orders, and he ruled without Parliament for the next 11 years.

During those 11 years, tensions grew. Unable to create taxes without Parliament, Charles extended the reach of seldom used laws, selling monopolies and taking back lands that had been given to Scottish nobles, all to fill his own coffers. This created anger and resentment throughout the country. Furthermore, religious tensions were also rising. Charles made Laud into the Archbishop of Canterbury in 1633, leading to attacks on Puritan religious practices. Those who did not confirm to official church doctrine were mutilated and imprisoned, creating martyrs for the independent religious cause.

Charles was King of Scotland as well as England, with the two separate countries having shared a monarch since his father, King James VI of Scotland, inherited the English throne as King James I. But Charles's high-handed approach to politics caused further trouble north of the border, and not just because of the lands he had taken back from the nobility. The Scots were Presbyterian Protestants, and Charles wanted to enforce the same religious practices on them as he supported in England. His attempt to enforce use of the English Book of Common Prayer led to a rebellion by the Scots in 1639, a rebellion which ultimately became known as the Bishops' Wars.

Wars were expensive to fight, and even the measures Charles had used throughout the 1630s could not fund a war to bring the Scots into line. Thus, in 1640, he reluctantly recalled Parliament, his sole purpose being to raise taxes. Cromwell made his second appearance in Parliament as the MP for Ely in this sitting. He was one of many Puritans voted in by electors who were less than enthusiastic about paying for a war to enforce religious practices they themselves opposed. Within a month, it was clear that Charles would not get the taxes he wanted, and Parliament was once again dissolved, earning it the nickname of the Short Parliament.

The King could make the English Parliament go away, but he could not do the same for the Scottish rebellion. Many Scottish soldiers were veterans of the bitter religious fighting in Europe, which was then in the middle of the Thirty Years War. After they beat the English at the Battle of Newburn on 28 August 1640 and occupied northern England, Charles was forced to make a humiliating peace, and then, adding insult to injury, he had to summon Parliament to raise money he had promised to the Scots in return for an end to the war.

This Parliament, which became known as the Long Parliament, first assembled on November 3, 1640. Cromwell was once again in its midst, this time as MP for Cambridge, a position probably gained through political patronage. He had moved with his family to London, where he was part of a Puritan political and religious network. This group, which included various MPs and the Earls of Essex, Warwick and Bedford, had a reforming agenda. They wanted to see regular Parliaments keeping the King in check and a greater degree of religious freedom.

Cromwell was now playing a more important role in politics. In the first week of the new Parliament, he presented a petition for the release from prison of John Lilburne, a famous Puritan agitator. In May 1641 he put forward the Annual Parliaments Bill for its second reading, one of the reformers' attempts to extend their authority through legislation. In the same month he and Henry Vane the Younger introduced one of the most radical proposals yet, the Root and Branch Bill, which sought to abolish the episcopacy and so create a less hierarchical church over which it would be harder for the monarch to assert control.

Though Parliament as a whole was not yet ready for such radical ideas, neither was it ready to give King Charles what he wanted. Of 493 MPs in the Long Parliament, over 350 opposed the king. In return for the funds he so desperately needed, it forced Charles to accept measures that prevented him from dissolving Parliament, as well as the execution of one of his key advisors and other measures loathsome to the monarch.

Charles's main political battleground might be England, but those battles were often triggered by events in the other countries he ruled. In October 1641, Irish Catholics revolted against Protestant English settlers, but while both sides in Parliament wanted to bring the rebels to heel, they argued over the funding and control of the army needed to do the job. More MPs supported Charles in the face of this outside threat, but enough opposed him for him to believe rumors that they planned to impeach his queen.

On January 4, 1642 Charles tried to arrest the leaders of the opposition in the chamber of Parliament. This exposed him as a despot, but also as a failure, since the six men escaped before Charles and his soldiers arrived. Cromwell witnessed firsthand an attempt to persecute the leaders of his political faction, men whose agenda he had supported and whose ideals he shared. Men who in his eyes were only seeking a better future for England.

Following the failed arrests, the country slid ever faster towards polarization and conflict. Charles fled London, which came under the control of Parliament, and both sides started raising armies, even as negotiations took place. Ultimately, there was to be no agreement; on August 22, 1642, Charles raised the royal standard at Nottingham and the First Civil War began.

The Civil Wars

The First Civil War, like so many civil conflicts, was fought not just between professionals but between enthusiastic amateurs, men determined to make their mark on the country. Oliver Cromwell was one such man. At the start of the war, Cromwell's only military experience was in the trained bands, local militias raised for purposes of defense, but as a member of the landed gentry, an MP and even a minor player in the politics leading up to the war, he had enough status and money to make an officer of himself. Like other men in similar positions, he raised troops to fight for the Parliamentary cause, in his case a cavalry troop from Cambridgeshire, and went to join the army.

Raising his cavalry troop was perhaps the first time that Cromwell was able to display the leadership skills which would make him so influential. Unlike some other officers, he successfully gathered a large troop of men, not just through his moderate wealth but through his personal influence. Indeed, while nobody could have foreseen it, this marked the beginning of a great military career.

The First Civil War was bitter, devastating and often close fought. Cromwell arrived too late to take part in the Battle of Edgehill, the war's first major engagement, on October 22, 1642, but Edgehill was not the decisive engagement both sides hoped for, and the war quickly spread. Cromwell's troop became a full regiment over the winter of 1642-3, and part of the Eastern Association, an organization of troops from England's eastern counties initially commanded by Baron Grey of Werke. As his title suggests, military leadership was a predominantly noble pursuit even in an armed struggle against the king.

Baron Grey of Werke

As a captain of horse, Cromwell soon started to make a name for himself by helping to prevent royalist advances south. With Hull threatened by the king's men in July, he was one of the officers sent to relieve a parliamentary position in the region. He took Burghley House and relieved the troops at Gainsborough on July 28, 1643 through a decisive and courageous cavalry action, but across the country the royalists were advancing, and without enough infantry to hold his position, Cromwell withdrew south.

Cromwell's capability as a commander led him to rise through the ranks, and when the Earl of Manchester took over the Eastern Association troops in August 1643, Cromwell was appointed Lieutenant General of the Horse. But while he was respected as a commander, he clashed with many of the men around him, including Manchester, due to his egalitarian and strongly Puritan opinions. Not everyone on the Parliamentary side held the same views on the future of England, divisions which would become significant after the war, and a traditionally-minded nobleman like Manchester, whose own position was reliant upon the existing social and political order, was not a good fit with a fire and brimstone Puritan like Cromwell.

From May-July 1644, the Eastern Association besieged the royalists holding Lincoln. Prince Rupert, a leading royalist commander, broke the siege on July 1 and then led his troops out to fight the parliamentary forces on July 2. What followed was the Battle of Marston Moor, in which Cromwell played a decisive part. Despite the success of Cromwell's cavalry on the left flank, the rest of the army almost went into retreat, pushed back by the royalists, but he rallied his battle-weary troops, got around behind the enemy lines and attacked them from the rear. The enemy flank was shattered, and the outnumbered royalists soon surrendered.

Two weeks later, York surrendered, leaving Parliament dominant in the war, but despite this decisive engagement, Parliament failed to capitalize on the victory. Without a strong central organization and leadership, the army failed to properly coordinate, leading to indecisive engagements and the surrender of one of its commanders. In October, King Charles escaped an encircling maneuver at the Second Battle of Newbury, a failure for which Cromwell blamed Manchester, leading to further disputes between the two men.

In the face of these failures, Parliament reformed its forces as the New Model Army, the first English army to be uniformly dressed in their distinctive red coats. These reforms towards a more professional army were embodied in the New Model Ordinance and the Self-Denying Ordinance passed by Parliament in early 1645, which reshaped the army on a national basis rather than leaving its organization to local bodies. The Ordinances also prevented Members of Parliament, whether lords like Manchester or MPs sitting in the House of Commons, from being military commanders, forcing them to choose between political and military power. Such was Cromwell's status that an exception was made for him and he retained both positions, but the rest gave up their military positions. Cromwell would no longer have to work with Manchester.

Cromwell played a leading role in the military reforms, and when the New Model Army set out on campaign in April 1645 he was its cavalry commander and second-in-command, under Sir Thomas Fairfax.

A portrait of Fairfax

Cromwell would now take a vital part in the most decisive battle of the First Civil War. The Battle of Naseby, fought on June 14, 1645, was a critical victory for the New Model Army. Prince Rupert's cavalry broke the parliamentary left flank and then went on to chase down the routed soldiers and attack their baggage train. However, Cromwell, having achieved dominance on the opposite flank, gathered his forces and rallied the broken parliamentary left. He and Fairfax then advanced their cavalry on the royalist infantry from both sides, bringing about a decisive victory and forcing thousands of men to surrender. Cromwell was later quoted as saying before the battle, "I could not, riding out alone about my business, but smile out to God in praises, in assurance of victory because God would, by things that are not, bring to naught things that are." Contemporary English writer John Aubrey referenced Cromwell's seemingly strange antics ahead of this battle and future ones: "One that I knew was at the battle of Dunbar, told me that Oliver was carried on with a Divine impulse; he did laugh so excessively as if he had been drunk; his eyes sparkled with spirits. He obtain'd a great victory; but the action was said to be contrary to human prudence. The same fit of laughter seized Oliver Cromwell just before the battle of Naseby; as a kinsman of mine, and a great favourite of his, Colonel J. P. then present, testified. Cardinal Mazerine said, that he was a lucky fool."

Although the war would run on for another year, it now became a mopping up operation. The

New Model Army had more men, better supplies, and higher morale, as well as the strategic advantage. They besieged and captured royalist strongholds, chased the royalists around the country, and undermined Charles's military support. He eventually handed himself over to the Scots, who had played their own independent part in the Civil War, often on the parliamentary side. The last substantial royalist stronghold of Oxford surrendered in June 1646. The fighting was not entirely over - Harlech in Wales held out as a royalist bastion until March 1647 - but the King had surrendered and the matter was decided.

Cromwell's impact on the war, and thus his future political standing, was based on his superiority as a cavalry commander. Like so many others in the war, he started out as an amateur, but he was a gifted one. Charismatic and determined, he was able to recruit more men than many other cavalry commanders and to keep them in order on the battlefield. Rather than the wild pursuits of Prince Rupert, which used the fury and momentum of a successful cavalry charge to run the routed enemy into the ground, Cromwell brought his men back into order after a success. This meant that they were more useful on the battlefield, not just chasing away enemies in skirmishes on the flanks but turning that advantage into superior numbers and flanking maneuvers on the enemy's infantry lines. Cromwell also changed the way that his men fought, using close order cavalry formations to give his charges more impact. The role of cavalry on the battlefield was changing across Europe at the time, and in Cromwell, Parliament was lucky to have a commander who adapted well to the changing face of war.

Over four bloody years, Oliver Cromwell had risen from a minor opposition politician into a leading figure of the national army. He and his ideological allies now controlled a country damaged by the divisions and devastation of war, but there was a peace to be built, and that would prove an equally difficult task.

Even after the First Civil War ended, the divisions were complex and the sides shifted over time, but they can be boiled down to two main viewpoints. On one side of the parliamentary movement were those who sought moderate levels of reform in order to lower the risk of a despotic king and a Catholic-influenced church. Dominant in Parliament, their preference was for reconciliation with Charles. Including many of the men who had led the country towards war, as well as those who had more reluctantly taken Parliament's side, they tried to put together a settlement in which everybody had a part. Charles would be restored while accepting certain constraints. The established Church of England would be replaced by a Presbyterian model like the Scottish church, a form of Protestantism in which the church was run by a body of elders rather than dictated to by a single leading figure.

On the other side were the radicals, men who held less sway in Parliament but were hugely influential in the New Model Army, where they often provided a voice for ordinary soldiers. Several different Protestant sects had emerged during the chaos of the First Civil War, when no one was able to undertake the traditional governmental duty of suppressing religious dissent. They combined radical political and religious views, these being one and the same in the 17th century mindset. Most eloquent and coherent were groups such as the Levellers and the Diggers, who pushed for levels of political and economic equality that were unthinkable to traditionalists. They sought religious freedom for Protestants so that they themselves could continue to worship as they saw fit, and opposed the imposition of a nationally aligned church, even a Presbyterian one.

These divisions were not purely ideological either. Many moderates wanted to disband the New Model Army now that the war was won, and this had practical consequences for the soldiers. They were still owed pay for having taken part in the risky business of war, and the army had provided them with a voice for the first time in their lives. An attack on the army was therefore also an attack on their interests.

Hanging over this were the specters of Catholicism and Scotland. Even the most radical Puritans did not want to see toleration extended to Catholics, though some in the country still secretly leaned that way. Meanwhile, the Scots, themselves armed and organized and theoretically subjects of the same king, were eager for a settlement that would favor their own political and religious interests.

Cromwell's sympathies lay more with the radicals of the New Model Army. These were his men, the ones who had fought and bled at his command, and they shared his Puritan faith and his distaste for anything with even a hint of Popery about it. At the same time, he was not an extreme hardliner; he was a member of the landed gentry and not interested in the radical social transformation sought by the Levellers.

Parliament's intention to disband the army with its wages unpaid led to a mutiny, during which the regiments elected Agitators to voice their concerns. Most of the officers, including Cromwell, sided with the mutineers. They seized the King, who at that time was held by Parliament, took control of London, and published a manifesto of their grievances and desired reforms. Cromwell had his son-in-law Henry Ireton put together a proposed package of reforms, the *Head of Proposals*. This aimed for a constitutional monarchy involving religious toleration, regular but reformed Parliaments, reduced power for bishops, and measures intended to prevent the King immediately rolling back the reforms.

Ireton

At the same time, there were many radical agitators in the army, men pushing for a more substantial change in the country than most MPs and the gentry officers of the New Model Army would ever endorse. These proposals were presented in two successive documents, *The Case of the Armie Truly Stated* and its successor *The Agreement of the People*. The radicals wanted more than just to use Parliament to curb the King. Having fought and bled for Parliament, they now wanted to be represented within it, with equal representation for all men in Parliament, rather than the existing system which only gave votes to a wealthy minority.

The Putney Debates, a series of meetings between army officers and representatives of the common soldiers, took place in October and early November 1647 with the aim of finding common ground between these two approaches to reform, both radical by the standards of the era and yet somehow at odds with each other. Cromwell took a leading part in these debates, chairing meetings, supporting the *Head of Proposals* and trying to achieve reconciliation. He used prayer as a way of creating bonds between men with very different views but a shared and fervent Protestant faith. In line with his own beliefs, he also encouraged all involved to seek guidance from God in their prayers. It was indicative of the challenge he faced that these men, who shared his strong faith in a personal relationship with the divine, could return to the meetings after a night of prayer with their opposing beliefs reinforced rather than reconciled. This radicalism showed no signs of abating with its flames fanned by agitators from outside the army, and Cromwell and Fairfax eventually came to see it as a form of mutiny. They gathered the army in a series of separate mass meetings, used force of will to achieve unity in place of divisive radicalism, and court-martialed nine leading mutineers.

Though he was a reformer and has gone down in history as the man who led the forces of representation against an authoritarian monarch, it would be a mistake to view Cromwell as a democrat in the modern sense. As the Putney Debates showed, he was a man with a deep sense of right and wrong, and one who was only so willing to listen to dissenting voices. He despised the tyranny he associated with Charles, but he did not see all men as equally worthy of participation in the business of running the country. He wanted leadership by a group of God-fearing, property-owning men who shared his Protestant convictions and who were as uncomfortable with the unruly mob as with an untrustworthy monarch. While radicals sought to do away with Charles, Cromwell sought a way to achieve a stable reconciliation with the King, though on more radical terms than those favored by his parliamentary colleagues.

It is a sign of just how badly King Charles misjudged his position that he went from this point, when Cromwell would execute his own men rather than end negotiations with the King, to a situation in which Cromwell played a leading part in having him executed. However, Charles was a schemer and a man who, against all evidence, seemed unable to recognize that events might not go his way. With Parliament and the New Model Army fractured on the question of where to take the peace, he played the two off against each other, all the while negotiating with a third party: the Scots. While the Putney debates were still ongoing, Charles escaped captivity and tried to flee to France. But the governor of the Isle of White, who Charles believed would assist him, instead imprisoned the King, and he found himself once again a captive of Parliament.

Unable to escape the country, he instead entered into a secret treaty with the Scots in December 1647. His new allies agreed to invade England in support of a royalist uprising the following year. This agreement was not made public until it was discussed in the Scottish Parliament in February, but it was clear to politicians in England that the king could not be trusted and that violence was once again impending. Defenses were prepared, and in February 1648 Parliament agreed by a majority of 80-50 on the Vote of No Addresses, a public declaration that they would no longer negotiate with the king. In doing this, and in justifying its position, Parliament arranged for pamphlets to be printed explaining and condemning Charles's duplicitous behavior, as well as listing the king's previous misdeeds. This turned public opinion further towards the radicals, galvanizing the country not just for war but for the changes that would follow it.

During the interim period between the two civil wars, the peace had seen Cromwell's position strengthened. He was the officers' prime mover in the Putney Debates and showed the common soldier that he would listen to their concerns, but that he would bring them into line if needed. Meanwhile his opponents were rushing down paths that would see them critically weakened. Charles wasted his opportunity for reconciliation under a constitutional monarchy, while Parliament failed in its dealings with him. As the country once again headed down a polarizing path towards violence, Oliver Cromwell was looking stronger than ever.

The willingness of the Scots to support Charles I in the Second Civil War, despite their previous alliance with Parliament, was motivated in part by what they saw of England's sectarian divisions and in part by what Charles himself had to offer. Despite the efforts of Cromwell and his allies to achieve unity, England had been torn apart ideologically during the first war, unleashing a wave of radical sects pulling the country in different directions. The Scottish nobility feared facing this sort of chaos in their own country, and they also worried that without the threat of the Royalist cause, the New Model Army might bring its disciplined troops and its religion north of the border in a new invasion. Charles played to these fears, holding out an alternative that conceded just enough to bridge the gap between an Arminian king and a Presbyterian country. In return for their support Charles would acknowledge the Scottish church as it stood and bring in Presbyterianism in England, though temporarily at first.

Meanwhile, the Puritanism of Cromwell and his colleagues was causing discontent, which also gave the royalists hope. In an attempt to stamp out anything that smelled even faintly of Catholicism and to impose serious, virtuous behavior on an unruly population, major holidays had been banned. Phallic looking Maypoles, drunken St George's Day revelries, celebrations of the King's accession to the throne, and other similar events were abolished. But the most serious blow was the banning of Christmas festivities, including decorations and days off work. Deprived of their opportunity for good cheer in the darkest part of the year, people rioted all across the country, most seriously in Kent. There violent protest turned into an armed rebellion.

The Second Civil War opened with terrible inevitability in late April 1648, with the occupation of Berwick and Carlisle in northern England by men gathered to fight for Charles's cause. In the southeast, men of Essex and Kent continued to defy Parliament, while south Wales, which had held out to the bitter end of the previous war, once more rose up for the king. Fairfax was sent to deal with the southeastern counties, eventually containing the rebels in Colchester, while risings in the southwest faltered. The duty of dealing with Wales was given to Cromwell.

Since its conquest by the English in the 13th century, Wales had been controlled by a serious of castles dominating towns along the coastline. Regaining control of the region was therefore a matter of retaking these castles. Though Cromwell's skills as a cavalry commander were unlikely to play a major role in this, he was by now recognized as a leading general and hence put in charge of the army that marched west.

As it turned out, the Welsh campaign was a short and successful one for Cromwell and one in which he proved less merciful than in the previous war. He captured Chepstow and Tenby in late May, burned down Carmarthen Castle, and moved on to besiege Pembroke Castle, the heart of the revolt. Isolated and faced with the might of the New Model Army, the castle surrendered on July 11, 1648. Cromwell was lenient towards longstanding royalists among the rebels but not towards those who had defected from the parliamentary side, and one of their leaders was eventually executed in London.

It took the Scots a couple of months to mobilize their army, so they didn't invade England until July 8. By then, royalists had seized Pontefract Castle and the Scarborough garrison had defected to the King, giving the rebels four strongholds in northern England. Aside from that, however, the country failed to rise up in revolt as Charles had hoped. A naval mutiny had been contained, the rebels in the southeast were cornered by Fairfax, and those in Wales were falling to Cromwell.

After capturing Pembroke, Cromwell took 4,000 of his men and marched north to face the Scots. He met with another small parliamentary army under John Lambert, with Cromwell taking overall command, and on August 17, they caught up with the larger Scottish army under the Duke of Hamilton, which was strung out along its route of march south, and defeated them in battle at Preston. Cromwell pressed hard against the retreating Scots and royalists, pursuing them relentlessly over the next week until the infantry had all been killed or surrendered and Hamilton had fled with the remnants of his cavalry.

The Battle of Preston ended any hopes of a royalist victory, but Colchester held out under siege throughout the summer. Civilians suffered from starvation, and the town was devastated by artillery bombardments. Both sides blamed each other for the horrors inflicted there and feared that England was slipping into the sort of brutality seen in the religious conflict of the Thirty Years War, then reaching its end on the continent.

If the rest of the country was polarized by the propaganda and politics leading up to the Second Civil War, Cromwell's views became polarized by the war itself. He came to agree with the radical preachers who blamed King Charles for the nation's woes. His was a politics built on faith, and he believed that the army's success showed that both King Charles and Parliament, which kept seeking compromise with the monarch, lacked real authority from God. Thus, there was now no doubt in Cromwell's mind that there could be no peace through compromise with Charles, and if Parliament could not realize this in its own wisdom, then it would fall to the army, blessed by God and led by righteous men like Cromwell and Ireton, to set them straight.

The Civil Wars were over, but the struggle for the future was not.

The Commonwealth and the Lord Protector

The fallout from the Second Civil War left Parliament in an awkward position. As a body it had previously made clear its unwillingness to depose Charles I, but the lead up to the second war had included a public declaration that it would no longer negotiate with the king. While many were unwilling to deal any longer with the scheming monarch, the majority of MPs also feared radical change, given its potential for social and political disruption. Even the arguments for launching the first war had centered around defending the traditional rights of Parliament and the propertied classes against the King's allegedly unprecedented and illegal tyranny, not a radical agenda of curbing royal power. However, while the majority of MPs were ready to repeal the Vote of No Addresses and return to negotiations with Charles, those who opposed negotiation were both larger in number and firmer in their convictions than ever before.

Among them was Cromwell. Parliament sent representatives to talk with the king at Newport, and by November they were on the verge of an agreement, with Charles's determined attachment to the power of bishops the only significant issue still in the way. But as in the period before the Second Civil War, the New Model Army's leaders and soldiers were more radical than Parliament. Even the officers in charge, conservative as they were compared with the Leveller agitators, were unhappy at the idea of retaining Charles as monarch. The division within the army was now over how to respond, with a group around Fairfax feeling that it was not the army's place to interfere in Parliament's business, while a group around Cromwell's son-in-law Ireton believed that they had a moral duty to prevent Charles returning to power. While heated debates took place in London, Cromwell stayed in the north with his army, avoiding having to take a side.

Parliament delayed discussing the Remonstrance, a document of Ireton's creation that set out the army's view that Charles should be tried as a criminal rather than negotiated with as a monarch. This delay finally pushed Fairfax into moving against Parliament in December 1648. He set firmer guards around Charles, ordered Cromwell to return to London, and mustered the army. Persuaded by friendly MPs not to completely dissolve Parliament, the army instead sent Colonel Thomas Pride to exclude moderates from Parliament on December 6-12, an event known as Pride's Purge. What remained - 200 MPs out of what had been 471 - is remembered as the Rump Parliament.

Ironically, it seems that Cromwell, though convinced of the need to get rid of Charles, hoped that he could be persuaded to abdicate in favor of his third son, Henry Duke of Gloucester, seen as less of an absolutist than his father. However, Charles would not consider this, and by Christmas Cromwell reluctantly accepted that a more radical approach was needed. Thus, on January 1, 1649, with encouragement from Cromwell, the Rump Parliament agreed to set up a High Court of Justice to try Charles for treason. Many people, Charles included, refused to cooperate with a trial whose legal standing was extremely questionable, but this great display still went ahead, starting on January 20 and ending on January 27, when the king was sentenced to death. Cromwell, Ireton and Pride were among the men who signed the death warrant. The king was executed on January 30, 1649, but it took two more months to decide who or what would take his place. The result was the declaration of the Commonwealth of England, a republic governed by the Rump Parliament and a smaller Council of State, which filled the executive role previously held by the king and royal council. Cromwell was a member of both bodies.

A depiction of the trial of King Charles I

An illustration depicting Cromwell leading the imprisonment of Charles I

Paul Delaroche's painting of Cromwell and the corpse of Charles I

Fairfax, who did not support the trial and execution of Charles, was withdrawing from public affairs, leaving Cromwell as the unchallenged leader of the army. His first task was to deal with Ireland, where royalists were gathering the support of Catholic rebels. However, in April 1649, as Cromwell was selecting the regiments to take with him, Levellers in the army started to protest against Parliament and the military leaders, who they saw as not radical enough in their agenda. This was meant to become a general uprising in May, and though it was never as successful as the organizers hoped, Cromwell and Fairfax had to lead forces into western England to put down the revolt. Along the way, they made promises to the rebels that they would dissolve the Rump and hold new elections, but these promises were never kept. In the end, the rebellion was not ended by negotiation but through a brief and bloody skirmish in mid-May which effectively ended the Leveller influence on politics.

Parliament had wanted to re-conquer Ireland since it rebelled in 1641, and Cromwell viewed the Irish rebels as a serious menace, both because of the deaths of many Protestants during previous revolts and because of their Catholicism, which he saw as a pernicious foreign influence and a deviation from true Christian faith. He arrived in Ireland in August 1649, shortly after the main rebel army had been defeated by another force. What remained was to besiege and capture rebel settlements, a task which he started on the east coast with the town of Drogheda. Though hugely outnumbered, the garrison in Drogheda refused to surrender. Cromwell responded with a bombardment on September 10 and an assault the next day, pushing into the town. When the garrison still refused to surrender, as it would normally have been expected to do, Cromwell ordered that anyone found with arms should be executed, not captured. The cornered soldiers were massacred, as were priests and some civilians, and though Cromwell never ordered the deaths of civilians, he later conceded, "I believe we put to the sword the whole number of the defendants. I do not think thirty of the whole number escaped with their lives…in the heat of the action, I forbade them to spare any that were in arms in the town".

Similar carnage took place when he captured Wexford the following month, after which New Ross surrendered rather than resist and face a massacre, but Waterford, which Cromwell besieged in November, held out. Cromwell eventually had to give up on this siege as his army suffered from winter diseases and poor weather, but by January 1650, Cromwell was back in the field, besieging and assaulting castles. He captured the rebel capital of Kilkenny on March 27, and the ineptitude of his opponents then led a large portion of the rebels to defect back to Parliament. The last substantial rebel stronghold was Clonmel, where thousands of New Model Army soldiers died due to a trap set by the garrison commander, but it ultimately capitulated in May.

By now, news had arrived that Charles I's son, the future Charles II, had signed an alliance with the Scots, so Cromwell left Ireton to mop up the Irish rebels and returned to England to face this new northern menace. That June, Parliament made Fairfax the official commander of the defense of northern England, with Cromwell once again as his second-in-command, but they also gave the order that this defense should take the form of a preemptive invasion of Scotland, and on June 22, Fairfax resigned rather than lead an invasion which he did not agree with. Cromwell could not dissuade him, so on June 28, the former cavalry commander was appointed as Lord General.

Charles II

Now in overall command of the New Model Army, Cromwell marched his troops north. The need to deal with Ireland and prevent rebellions in England meant that the Scottish invasion army was constantly low on supplies, suffering from disease and malnutrition, and they initially struggled with a strong Scottish defensive line. Besieged by the numerically superior Scots at Dunbar, Cromwell ordered a night attack, even though most of his commanders advised him to withdraw. By exploiting a weakness in the Scottish line, he was able to outmaneuver his opponents, achieving a crushing victory in which 4,000 Scottish soldiers were killed and 10,000 captured.

A painting depicting Cromwell at Dunbar

Cromwell went on to conquer Edinburgh, where he showed far more mercy than he had in Ireland. He wanted to dislodge the Scottish leaders who had pushed for war and integrate Scotland peacefully into English territory, so massacres were out of the question. Instead, he launched a two-pronged assault into western Scotland in November, in which the Scottish army was smashed by English commander John Lambert. An attempt to seize the Fife in February 1651 ended in failure for Cromwell and he became seriously sick, but his opponents were too divided to make the most of the Lord General's convalescence.

Following further successes for Cromwell and Lambert in June and July, Cromwell deliberately left the way open for Charles to invade England. Charles rose to the bait, after which he was pursued by Cromwell and most of his troops. English cavalry harassed the Scots on their way south, a reminder of the devastating pursuit of the last Scottish invasion. Charles tried to rally royalists at Worcester, but few flocked to his banner and he was thoroughly defeated by Cromwell. Almost the entire army surrendered, with Charles himself one of the very few to escape.

With the Civil Wars over, Cromwell encouraged the Rump Parliament to follow his reforming agenda and create a new constitution to fill the gap left by the king. He wanted to see the countries of England (including long-conquered Wales), Scotland and Ireland brought together in a single political body with a national church that tolerated different Protestant observances, and he wanted fresh parliamentary elections. However, while it introduced some religious toleration, the Rump failed to bring about substantial reforms such as replacing existing church tithes, and did not set a date for the election that would see it replaced. It also angered many men in the army by ordering the seizure of royalist estates; though the army had fought hard against the royalists, it had also encouraged their surrender by promising not to seize these lands, so Parliament's actions undermined the honor and intentions of the army.

Though both the army and the Rump were divided, the gap between the two bodies was greater, and army officers started encouraging Cromwell to step in and deal with Parliament's failings. On April 18-19, 1653, he met with his officers and parliamentary allies, creating a proposal for Parliament to replace itself with a temporary governing body of forty men. However, on April 20, news arrived that Parliament, rather than debate this proposal, was debating its own different bill. Cromwell went to Parliament, took his seat, listened to the debate as long as he could tolerate, and then rose to his feet. He gave an angry speech against the failings of the Rump, called in soldiers, and dispersed Parliament.

After that, Cromwell convened a new Council of State, whose purpose was to set up a new body to govern the country. This Nominated Assembly consisted of men chosen by the army for their righteous religious beliefs, fitting Cromwell's views that the country should be run by the godly, and it first met on July 4. He gave the Assembly until November 1654 to establish a body to replace itself, which would in turn produce a permanent constitution. However, the Nominated Assembly, popularly known as the Barebones Parliament after one of its most radical members, was sharply divided between radical and moderate reformers who could agree on absolutely nothing. By November, it was clear that the assembly was not working, and on December 12, the moderates resigned in bunches, brought in soldiers to prevent the remaining assembly from sitting, and went to Cromwell asking him to replace the assembly with a new constitution. Two parliaments had now failed in the space of a single year, and a different form of leadership was needed.

Mid-17th century portrait of Cromwell

On two occasions, Cromwell had tried to create a collective body to make decisions, only to see it dissolved at gunpoint, so he now accepted what he had so long resisted: a country run by one man, that man being him. On December 15, the Instrument of Government, a constitution drafted by John Lambert, was adopted. The Instrument was based on the principle that power needed to be balanced between different bodies to prevent despotism, whether by a sole ruler or a corrupt assembly, but Lambert also recognized that assemblies and parliaments could not act quickly and decisively, and that such decisiveness was sometimes needed. Thus, three branches of government were set up : a large legislative Parliament, a small executive Council, and a Lord Protector who oversaw and was limited by both. Parliament was reformed in the process, and both Catholics and Royalists were excluded to prevent a new Parliament that would vote the monarchy back in.

John Lambert

On December 16, 1653, under the provisions of the Instrument, Cromwell was sworn in as Lord Protector of the Commonwealth of England, Scotland and Ireland. The title of Lord Protector had previously been used by those acting as regents in the absence of a monarch, but now it became the title for the man permanently replacing the king. Though he wore his familiar plain black clothes rather than grandiose royal regalia for the swearing in ceremony, what followed had the familiar governmental form of a monarchy. Cromwell could call and dissolve Parliament, received a very large income from the nation, and continued to control his ever-loyal army. He could veto laws, though this power was limited, and he ran the Council. Church bells were rung following his investiture, and he was even being spoken to as "Your Highness."

One of the most significant novelties of Cromwell's regime was that he was the first English ruler to have a permanent standing army. The New Model Army, as a reformed and professional body, had replaced local militias and armies raised on the basis of need. It was fiercely attached to Cromwell, who had led it through war, reform and spectacular victories. This gave him greater power in practice even than that given to him by the new constitution.

The most urgent issue to be addressed was making peace with the Dutch. A war had recently broken out over control of trade, a war in which Cromwell played no part because it was fought at sea, but both sides were tiring of the war, and in April 1654 peace was made, a goal in which Parliament's negotiators had previously failed. In developing diplomatic relations with other countries, the Lord Protector adopted the pomp and circumstance of formal receptions for ambassadors, something abandoned since Charles's fall. This was done to meet the expectations of these visitors and assert English authority, but it also reinforced Cromwell's position as a proxy king. Whether such grandeur was needed is questionable since other European states, very aware of the military power with which Cromwell had laid waste to the ambitions of Charles, Ireland, and Scotland, all rushed to establish good relations with England's new ruler.

Since Cromwell's return to London as a general in 1650, he and his family had been living in accommodation attached to the Palace of Whitehall. The Palace itself was now given to them as their home, setting them up in the sort of grandeur expected of a head of state. They were given a household of servants and entertainers, many of whom had previously served the king, and the staffing of the Protector's household increasingly came to resemble a royal one. Half a dozen other royal residences, including Windsor Castle, were also made available to him.

In keeping with his Puritan character, Cromwell accepted these monarchical trappings as a necessary part of maintaining the authority of the head of state, rather than seeking out such extreme privilege. Some saw this as Cromwell putting on a show of humility, but he was a deeply religious man, wedded to a more egalitarian faith than that of Charles I. If he had really wanted such status and grandeur, it would have been his for the taking years before, given the power he wielded in the country. The fact was that, culturally as well as politically, England and the other nations it had conquered were not ready to do without a single central leader of great authority and status. Despite the protestations of the Levellers and other radicals, Charles's execution left a void, and Cromwell was brought in to fill it.

Cromwell and the Council sought peace at home as well as abroad by trying to unify their previously separate countries. National Parliaments were replaced by Scottish and Irish seats in what had previously been the English Parliament, and other measures were taken to reconcile their people.

In these ways, the new government set about trying to return the country to some kind of stability after the terrible upheavals of the Civil Wars, a policy Cromwell labeled "healing and settling." He rejected the revolutionary social and political reforms favored by Parliamentary radicals and the more extreme religious groups, but in this regard, he faced a struggle with Parliament, which met in its new form for the first time in September 1654. It almost immediately set about challenging the authority of the military-led government and preparing a new constitution. This was not the acquiescent body that Cromwell had looked for after the closure of the last two Parliaments, so he dissolved it in January 1655.

With that action, the tripartite political balance of the Instrument of Government was falling apart, and a failed royalist uprising in March 1655 gave Cromwell an excuse to re-examine the way that the country was governed. Influenced once again by Lambert, the Protectorate's great political philosopher, Cromwell divided England up into 15 military districts. These were governed by Army Major Generals, responsible for maintaining troops, raising taxes and ensuring support for the government. The Major Generals also pushed Cromwell's agenda of Puritan religious reform, with the assistance of commissioners in each county. This system of devolved military dictatorship lasted less than a year, being voted out by a later Parliament, but its short lived activities reopened old wounds and stirred up opposition to the new regime, opposition which would eventually turn into support for the restored monarchy.

Despite his outspoken opposition to both public Catholicism and religious reform more radical than his own, Cromwell believed in freedom of conscience in private worship, and he acted to make this a reality. Hoping to tap into their wealth, he encouraged Jews to return to England after many of them had fled the intolerance of previous regimes. Given his hope for a reformed religious community, Cromwell believed that the Jews would eventually turn to Christianity, but he did not try to enforce this, and compared with much of England's previous history, this was a tolerant period for them.

That said, while he accepted religious freedom in private, Cromwell did not want to see it enacted in public. Puritan moral reforms continued, such as the banning of pagan-looking Christmas festivals that had so recently led to riot and revolt. Where moral character was concerned, Cromwell's pragmatism would only stretch so far.

This approach to religious reform is indicative of the problem at the heart of Cromwell's religious and political thinking, a problem he faced at every turn. A man of deeply held convictions, he believed that a more egalitarian church and state, in which more people were able to participate, was the best bulwark against both political and religious tyranny. Indeed, such egalitarianism was needed in order to give people the freedom to behave in a more godly and upstanding fashion, free from the corrupting influence of bishops and decadent royals. But once they were given that freedom and participation, people failed to live up to the standards Cromwell looked for in them. They embraced frivolousness and drunkenness on public holidays, and they elected radicals and royalists. Instead of becoming good Puritans, they turned against the principles which, in Cromwell's eyes, would set them free.

It was this problem that led Cromwell to become Lord Protector, and that led to solutions such as local government by Major Generals. If people would not do right by choice, then he was willing, when pushed, to lead them to it, but even Cromwell, who had risen from obscurity through his strength of personality, could not make the horse drink. This was shown when Parliament once again met in September 1656. By now, England was at war with Spain, its traditional Catholic enemy, and Cromwell and his advisers hoped that this shared external threat would win Parliament around to their side. Nonetheless, while MPs voted in new funds to fight the war, they also ended the authority of the Major Generals and undermined the policy of religious toleration by persecuting the Quaker James Nayler.

A depiction of Nayler with a "B" branded onto his forehead for blasphemy

This is not to say that Cromwell lacked support in this Parliament, support he had guaranteed by excluding a hundred of the most disruptive members from the moment it first sat. There had long been rumors that he would be made king, and this issue was openly discussed in Parliament in January 1657. The House eventually voted by 123-62 to offer him the crown, and on March 31, this request was made official, but the Humble Petition and Advice did not just ask Cromwell to become king; it also asked him to restore a constitution similar to that which existed before the Instrument of Government. Many people supported this change, given its potential to reduce Cromwell's dominance of Parliament while restoring the comforting familiarity of monarchy, but many also opposed it, including radicals outraged at the idea of restoring the monarchy. Unsurprisingly John Lambert, the author of the Instrument of Government, opposed the dissolution of the settlement he had crafted, and the Humble Petition and Advice marked the end of his period of great influence.

Cromwell himself was deeply divided, torn again by circumstances which put his own principles in conflict. He recognized Parliament as expressing the will of the people, and the importance of listening to this will. He also recognized the practical value of a grand head of state. But he also believed that God had led him to destroy the monarchy, and he could not in good conscience go against this. Thus, after six weeks of wrestling with his conscience and debating with other worthies, Cromwell accepted most of the proposals set out in the Humble

Petition, but the one that he rejected was the one which everyone had been talking from the moment he became Lord Protector: the title of king.

A satirical cartoon depicting the Lord Protector usurping the power of kings

On June 26, 1657, Cromwell was given a new public investiture as Lord Protector, one as grand as any coronation ceremony, and those seeking the stability of monarchy now seemed to have what they wanted: a king in all but name. He created hereditary peers, had coins made bearing his image and sought out noble husbands for his daughters. Cromwell had solved his crisis of conscience by disassociating the nature of kingship from its title, thereby rejecting the latter while accepting the former.

A 1658 coin depicting the Lord Protector

When Parliament reconvened in January 1658, it was in its new form, but one which was remarkably similar to the old form from before the Protectorate. Two Houses were once more in place: the Lords, referred to at this time as the "Other House," and the Commons. There was no interference in the election of MPs to the Commons, and thus the troublemakers excluded from the previous Parliament once again took their seats. Once again, however, these republican radicals immediately set about challenging the shape of the new constitution, beginning with the title and authority of the Other House. The ensuing dispute prevented any work getting done and threatened yet more political upheaval, so on February 4, after just 10 days, Cromwell dissolved yet another Parliament.

The Restoration

An unfinished portrait of Cromwell by Samuel Cooper

1658 was a period of tragedy for Cromwell. Several close family members died, including his daughter Elizabeth in August. Already ill himself, he personally tended to Elizabeth as she lay dying, and he was devastated by the loss. But the worst was yet to come, for within a month, the Lord Protector himself would be dead.

By the summer of 1658, Cromwell was an increasingly sickly man, suffering from urinary or kidney complaints and a bought of malaria. The struggles to maintain a functioning government cannot have helped his health, and the death of his daughter Elizabeth capped his decline. He died on September 3, 1658, most likely from a bout of septicemia following a urinary infection. The date of his death was also the anniversary of two of his great successes: the battles of Dunbar and Worcester. Cromwell was buried at Westminster Abbey, and if that was not royal enough for the republican ruler, the ceremony was based on that used for King James I.

Chris Nyborg's picture of Cromwell's death mask at Warwick Castle

It is not clear who Cromwell intended to follow him as Lord Protector, and the issue was disputed both by contemporaries and by historians. He may have had his son-in-law Charles Fleetwood in mind, he may have intended through his inaction to nominate no one to follow him, or he may have been preparing his son Richard for the role. Regardless, those around him immediately leapt at the solution that best fit the proxy monarchy of the protectorate by making Richard Cromwell the Lord Protector.

Richard was the third of Oliver and Elizabeth Cromwell's four sons, but by the time of Oliver's death, he was the eldest surviving son. Aside from family connections, however, he was nothing like his the man he succeeded. He lacked his father's political and military inclinations, did not fight in the Civil Wars (though his older brother Oliver was a parliamentary officer and died of typhoid fever while serving in the army), and his political activity was mostly limited to his home county of Hampshire, where he was a Justice of the Peace and took part in local committees. National political influence could have been his for the taking - his younger brother Henry became an MP in 1653 - but he instead retained a more humble station until the first and second Protectorate Parliaments, in which he sat as an MP.

Nonetheless, following the reforms of the Humble Petition, Oliver had involved Richard more in politics. He attended the second investiture ceremony in June 1657, was appointed Chancellor of Oxford University in July, and joined the Council of State in December. Accepting the Humble Petition had made Cromwell responsible for selecting his successor, and he was at least testing Richard's potential for the role.

It is therefore not surprising that Richard found himself as Lord Protector after Oliver's death, but it is also not surprising to find that this humble man lacked the character to hold together a government of uncertain rules and questionable legitimacy, as his father had done since the Civil Wars. Parliament was recalled to deal with the government's debts and met in January 1659, and once again, disputes immediately broke out between moderate Presbyterians, radical reformers and closet royalists. Parliament also fell out with the New Model Army, which felt it was not being paid enough respect and feared that Parliament might disband it to avoid further costs. In April, military officers petitioned the Lord Protector for higher taxation to cover army expenses. They had no respect for Richard, who lacked his father's military background, and were now playing their own game, but Parliament ignored the petition and, remembering the army's interventions to exclude members from Parliament and dissolve previous meetings, passed resolutions to limit meetings by army officers and force them all to swear an oath not to subvert Parliament.

To this, the army responded in predictable fashion, assembling in London and forcing the unhappy Richard Cromwell to dissolve the current Parliament and recall the pro-army Rump Parliament. However, this was as far as cooperation between Richard and the army would ever go; the officers agreed to pay off his debts and provide him with a pension, in return for which he resigned as Lord Protector on May 25, 1659. He lived abroad for most of the next 20 years before returning to live in obscurity in England until his death on July 12, 1712.

What followed was the collapse of everything that Oliver Cromwell had struggled for over the last two decades. The army, Parliament and the citizens of London grappled with each other for control of the country, and even the army no longer remained a united political force. Civil war almost broke out again as a force under Lambert failed to prevent General Monck, the military governor of Scotland, from marching south and dissolving the Rump Parliament. Excluded MPs were restored on condition that they themselves dissolve Parliament, and following fresh elections without military intervention, a new Parliament met on April 25, 1660. Dominated by Presbyterians and Royalists, it accepted a settlement offered by the man titling himself Charles

II, the son and heir of Charles I. On May 25, 1660, Charles II returned to England, and less than two years after Cromwell's death, his work was undone with the restoration of the monarchy.

Cromwell's story is one of the most extraordinary in English history. At his lowest ebb, he was struggling with the emotional darkness of depression, defeated in the petty realm of local politics, and found much of his little wealth gone. Two decades later, he was the ruler of England, feared and respected throughout Europe, and living in a palace while his daughters married noblemen in grand stately ceremonies.

However, the legacy which concerned him was not his personal triumphs but the constitutional changes he had wrought by removing a despotic and Catholic-inclined king, reforming the army, state and church. Most of these reforms were undone shortly after his death, and the returning King Charles II heaped ignominy upon defeat by having Cromwell's body dug up and posthumously executed. Cromwell's body was then decapitated, as was Ireton's, and their heads were placed on a pike above Westminster Hall, where Charles I had been tried, for several years. To this day, there are still debates over the location of Cromwell's head, and whether it is actually in someone's private possession.

A contemporary depiction of the posthumous executions of Cromwell, John Bradshaw, and Ireton

Despite the restoration, however, and despite the fact England's republican experiment barely outlasted Cromwell, the Commonwealth and Restoration were hugely important in asserting the power of Parliament, and it permanently shifted England's political balance firmly towards a constitutional monarchy limited by Parliament. The Stuart monarchy was restored on condition of compromise with Parliament and the army, and a precedent had been set for Parliament to replace the monarch, a precedent it would follow in the 1680s when James II was replaced by William and Mary in a settlement that set even more limits around the monarch. In that sense, Oliver Cromwell, who was king in all but name, helped prepare the way for monarchs who would become national leaders in name only.

On the religious front, Puritanism would never become the dominant form of religious and political thought that Cromwell wanted. His efforts to enforce its strictures did as much to turn people against the Puritans as to convert them, and Cromwell never appreciated that most of the ordinary English were not looking for moral direction but instead looking for life to be made easier and for the freedom to get drunk and celebrate Christmas. In fact, those with strict religious inclinations would have more impact in the New World than at home. The English church would soon restore much of its pomp and tradition, and English culture would once again embrace maypoles and noisy public holidays.

King James II and William of Orange

On October 14, 1633, the royal chambers of St. James's Palace erupted with the first cries of the royal newborn. The baby boy was to be named after his grandfather, and was soon introduced to the English public as James II. Queen Henrietta Maria, exalted but exhausted, held her baby in her arms, cooing lovingly at her creation. The nagging pain of the miscarriage she had suffered just 4 years ago, where she had lost her son, Charles James, slowly ebbed, and her heart swelled with joy and sweet relief. With her husband, England's very own King Charles I, she would have 6 more surviving children: Charles II; Henrietta; Mary, Princess Royal; Anne; Henry Stuart, Duke of Gloucester; and Elizabeth Stuart.

Tony Hisgett's picture of the St. James's Palace

Young James II with his father, Charles I of England

A few months after James was born, he was baptized by William Laud, the Anglican Archbishop of Canterbury. From an early age, James and his older brother, Charles II, were given daily lessons by a hand-picked selection of the nation's finest private tutors. On James's 3rd birthday, he was appointed the honorary title of Lord High Admiral, but would later take up the title as an adult. At age 11, young James was officially made the Duke of York.

Having grown up in the opulently decorated red-bricked towers and lavish courtyards of the Palace, it was safe to say that James was far more blessed than most when it came to his childhood. Unfortunately, that smooth life of luxury came skidding to a halt. In 1642, the "Roundheads" (Parliamentarian rebels against King Charles I) and the "Cavaliers" (monarchists) faced off in a violent chain of armed conflicts and political upheavals that lasted 9 years, otherwise known as the English Civil War. English Protestants had never been too keen on the king, who they held a grudge against for marrying the Catholic Henrietta Maria, as well as his retaliatory disbanding of Parliament on multiple occasions.

During the siege of Oxford in 1646, Parliamentarian leaders placed the Duke of York under house arrest. There he remained for 2 years, until royalist colonel Joseph Bampfield snuck into St. James's Palace. There, James donned a wig and a dress and was smuggled out of the palace and into the Hague in Netherlands.

16-year-old James was clocked with a second blow of terrible news; his father had been captured by Parliamentarians and tried in high court, where he was found guilty of treason. In early 1649, the king was beheaded. James's brother, Charles II, was declared king by the

Cavaliers, but would fail to get his hands on the English crown until later. For the meantime, he fled to France.

King Charles II of England

James also sought refuge in France, and it was there that he had his first taste of the battlefield when he joined the French army, but he would later cross over to the Spanish side in 1656. When he joined the Spanish army, he struck up a close friendship with a pair of Irish Catholic brothers. By 1660, the conflicts had simmered down, and his brother was formally crowned the king of England.

When James returned home that year, eyebrows around England shot up as the king's brother announced his engagement to Anne Hyde. People began to whisper about the choice since she was nothing more than a commoner, the simple daughter of Charles's chief minister. No one approved of the peculiar pairing, and for weeks, their loved ones badgered them, urging them not to proceed with the wedding. Queen Henrietta's skin crawled with the idea of her son marrying "beneath him." Even Anne Hyde's own father attempted to talk his daughter out of the marriage.

Nevertheless, in early September of that year, the lovebirds eloped. Anne Hyde gave birth to their first son, Charles, less than 60 days later, but he, along with 5 of his future siblings, never made it past their 2nd birthdays. Only 2 of their daughters would survive – Mary, and a younger sister who shared the same name with their mother, Anne.

Anne Hyde

In spite of his sacred vows, historians have often hinted at James's wandering eye, painting the philanderer as "the most unguarded ogler of the time." Like many other monarchs, he more than tainted the sanctity of marriage with his side collection of mistresses. James had a particular thing for "plain," slender Catholic maidens in their teens, including Arabella Churchill, Catherine Sedley, and 9 other young ladies.

Before Anne Hyde's death in 1671, James and his wife began to stray from their Anglican faith, and explored the Catholic Church. In 1669, 36-year-old James was said to have taken communion in a Roman Catholic Church, though this was kept under wraps. He carried on the Anglican facade for a few more years, attending Anglican services and mingling with Anglicans and Protestants, including John Churchill, the brother of one of his mistresses.

In 1672, King Charles II signed the Royal Declaration of Indulgence, otherwise known as the "Declaration for Liberty of Conscience." This suspended all penalties targeted at those outside the Protestant Church of England and granted Catholics and other non-Protestants the right to worship freely. This religious freedom was short-lived, however, as members of Parliament criticized their new king and named him a Catholic sympathizer. The horrendous fate of his father still fresh on his mind, Charles canceled the declaration the next year.

   In 1673, Parliament established the Test Act of 1673, and present and aspiring members of office and the military were now required to swear an oath to the monarch and the Protestant Church of England. In the same breath, they were to denounce the Catholic doctrine of transubstantiation, which was the transformation of bread and wine to the real body and blood of Christ during the sacrament of the Eucharist, which the English Protestants branded "superstitious and idolatrous." That same year, James refused this oath and stepped down from his post as Lord High Admiral. There were gasps from every corner of the country; the king's own brother, the Duke of York, was a Catholic. The humiliated king was furious, demanding that his nieces, 11-year-old Mary and 8-year-old Anne, follow tradition and be raised as Protestants. "Under fear of their being taken away from him altogether," James reluctantly agreed. When asked about his change of heart, James held up his chin and replied, "The divisions among Protestants and the necessity of an infallible judge to decide controversies, together with some promises which Christ made to his church in general...there being no person that pretends to infallibility but the Bishop of Rome."

   Later that year, Charles found himself exasperated again when James became engaged to an Italian princess, the Catholic Mary of Modena. He was hopelessly smitten with the stunning princess, described as a milk-skinned beauty with jet-black hair and eyes "so full of light and sweetness." This beauty had also come with brains, as the young girl could write in both Latin and French, and she had great interest and talent in music and art. Charles grumbled about it, but ultimately he gave his brother and sister-in-law-to-be his blessings. In late September of 1673, James tied the knot once more with his new 15-year-old bride.

   Yet again, these wedding bells brought nothing but obligatory rounds of halfhearted congratulations. Some kept a vigilant eye on the new Duchess of York, who they believed was a spy or a secret agent of sorts that had been dispatched by the pope himself. In fact, the infamous Popish Plot that would arise 5 years later only further stirred the simmering pot.

Mary of Modena

   1677 proved to be a particularly difficult year for James, one that came with a karmic twist. King Charles II arranged for the marriage between James's favorite daughter, 15-year-old Mary, and 27-year-old Protestant, William III. As rough as it was for James, it was said to have been worse for young Mary. Apart from being forced to take part in a marriage that the teenager had never asked for, William III was her first cousin, the son of James's sister Mary, Princess Royal. Mary was said to have burst into tears at the first sight of her unattractive cousin, a feeble, waxy-faced man with beady eyes, a bulky nose, and a crooked back. Her younger sister, Anne, stood by her sobbing sister's side, rather unkindly comparing her new brother-in-law to Prince Calibos (a mythological but grotesque swamp creature that had been cursed with deformity by the Greek god Zeus).

Mary

William III of Orange

As an interesting side note, some historians claim that Mary was a lesbian. From the age of 9 to 15, Mary wrote "passionate" letters with alleged romantic undertones to an older girl she idolized, Frances Apsley. Later, Apsley would also be Mary's maid of honor. Having said that, most historians dismiss the claim as rubbish. Others have also questioned the true nature of Anne's true sexuality.

James was said to have initially objected to the Protestant marriage, but after a bit of arm-twisting from his brother and other influential members of Parliament, the Duke of York conceded. Needless to say, the wedding, which took place in early November of that year, was anything but pretty. Mary's wedding dress was stained with the tears teeming down her face as she stood by the visibly uncomfortable William, while a poker-faced but nervous James watched the ceremony. King Charles was supposedly the only one in genuinely good spirits, all smiles as he cracked jokes back and forth, hoping to ease the tension. Unbeknownst to those present, the fidgety, unassuming groom would one day make a name for himself, in ways no one could have ever imagined.

William III of Orange was born in the Hague on November 4, 1650. While in his mother's womb, his father, William II, Prince of Orange and the stadtholder of the Netherlands, fell ill with smallpox and lost the battle against the debilitating disease. One week later, William II's grieving wife, Mary, went into labor, garbed from head to toe in soulless black. At age 9, young

William would lose his mother to the same wretched disease.

William II of Orange

William III had always been a sickly child, remembered by those in his time as a gaunt, asthmatic tyke born with a curved spine that gave him a faint hunchback. That said, William was an exceptionally bright child, and even with his physical shortcomings – or perhaps, as a product of them – the shrewd and patient William was determined to achieve greatness. Brothers Jan and Cornelius De Witt had assumed power of stadtholder after his father's death, and William was willing to go to any lengths to reclaim that title.

In an early display of William's cunning and persistence, he rolled up his sleeves and took advantage of the education at his disposal. With the help of Calvinist tutors, William learned the ins and outs of history, politics, and war. Along the way, he would not only pick up but master 4 different languages.

In 1672, the persistence of William and the Orangist party paid off. The public criticized the De Witt brothers for their failure to protect Flanders from French King Louis XIV's invading forces, and the pair were soon out of their post. In July that year, 22-year-old William was promoted from captain general to stadtholder, and the next month, the De Witt brothers were murdered by an angry mob.

Louis XIV

William's reign as stadtholder would be turbulent, particularly during the Dutch Wars from 1672 to 1678. He suffered great wins and devastating losses, and at times he squared off against armies of men 5 times his size, but William persevered. Throughout these years, he also managed to form close bonds with the leaders of Denmark, Brandenburg, and Spain. He would even experience a near brush with death when he was diagnosed with smallpox, made worse by a badly infected arm wound, but unlike his parents, he won that battle.

Though William and Mary's marriage had appeared doomed from the get-go, the pair would eventually grow to not only respect but love one another. This was not just a relationship based on an unlikely romance, it was a partnership that thrived on their shared drive for power and status. Soon, this dynamic power couple would ever so quietly paddle up to the surface and blow everyone out of the water.

As fate would have it, James was right to have second thoughts about the marriage after all.

Broken Promises

"If by the mere force of numbers a majority should deprive a minority of any clearly written constitutional right, it might, in a moral point of view, justify revolution." – President Abraham Lincoln, "First Inaugural Address"

Unfortunately for James, his daughter's Protestant marriage would pale in comparison to what was in store for him. Other than the hysteria that had been charged by the Popish Plot a year after William and Mary exchanged their vows, which further turned the Protestant public against the Catholics, James became the subject of an exclusion campaign. Panic began to rise on the Protestant side when after 16 years of marriage, King Charles II, and his wife, Catherine of Braganza, bore no live children. While Charles reportedly had 12 illegitimate children by a range of voluptuous mistresses, some of them sons, none of these bastard sons would ever have a chance at the throne, and the Protestants would not accept a Catholic king on the throne in the form of James should something happen to Charles.

Thus, the Earl of Shaftesbury, an ex-government minister and one of the most vocal opponents of the Catholic Church, fought to have James personally excluded from the throne in a formal Exclusion Bill. James took this up with his brother. He lamented, "Matters were come to such a head that the monarchy must be either more absolute or quite abolished."

In 1679, as Parliament threatened to pass the Exclusion Bill, the king took a stand. For the sake of his brother, he dissolved Parliament. 2 more parties of Parliament were formed in the next 2 years, but these were again knocked down at the slightest mention of the hotly contested Exclusion Bill. The quarreling sides split by the messy exclusion dilemma would help give rise to 2 political parties – the "Tories," who sided with the monarch in opposing the bill, and the "Whigs," the Parliamentarian rebels who supported it.

This Exclusion Bill would never be passed, but a discouraged James, hoping to shun the dreaded spotlight, retired to a lesser governmental post and made himself scarce. James later left for Brussels and would only return to England during dire times, including when his brother fell ill. Eventually, the Catholic panic began to dissipate, but there remained a perpetual rift between James and the Protestant Parliament.

As things were playing out around this time, on October 12, 1678, Sir Edmund Berry Godfrey, an esteemed Justice of the Peace, was brutally murdered. Godfrey was found face-down and sprawled out in a ditch, his own sword thrust deep into his lifeless corpse. Investigators later examined the battered body and reported he had a number of bruises and a strange, circular mark around his neck that indicated strangulation. Oddly, the bloodless wound of his sword suggested that it had been plunged into him hours after his death. Even more curious, there were no signs of a struggle near the crime scene, and though his body had been in the ditch for over 96 hours, his leather belt-wallet was still plump with cash and the winking rings on his fingers untouched. This was not a robbery gone wrong; there was clearly more to the case than met the eye.

Godfrey

A series of men would eventually be rounded up to pay for the crime. A day before Christmas, a Catholic servant named Miles Prance confessed to being one of the alleged conspirators, and he coughed up the names of the supposed masterminds: 3 Catholic priests. All 3 men of the cloth were apparently present during the murder, but those with actual blood on their hands were another trio of working men named Henry Berry, Robert Green, and Lawrence Hill. The 3 men were arrested and hanged in Primrose Hill in February of 1679.

This startling event shook the already hysterical masses. Just a month before the murder, a man by the name of Titus Oates had been summoned by the deceased to swear an oath on his testimony before it was presented to the king. The grim-faced magistrate listened as Oates relayed a terrible plot woven together by a rogue band of rebellious Catholics which had been drawn up during a secret Jesuit meeting in the White Horse Tavern of London. According to Oates, these rebels planned to assassinate King Charles II and replace him with his Catholic brother, James II. Oates recounted convincing details of possible methods that had made an appearance on the drawing board. One rebel suggested employing Irish mercenaries to stab the king in his slumber. One suggested an ambush by armed Jesuit soldiers. Another proposed a more subtle tactic by poisoning the monarch with the aid of the Queen's own personal physician.

Oates' sensational accusations only fueled the Catholic resentment that was already festering within the English community. The idea of colluding Catholics conniving to take over England was was not difficult to swallow; just 12 years before, in early September of 1666, a relentless fire was sparked in the home of King Charles' baker and would soon spread throughout London, running wild for 4 days before the fire was finally extinguished by authorities. By then, 80% of the city lay in smoldering ruins. The blame was passed around until it ultimately landed on the Catholics, who were accused of an act of religious terrorism. Despite the fact that authorities openly disproved this theory, the animosity the public had towards the Catholics intensified.

Oates would tell the story of the great plot to anyone who would listen. Soon, that was exactly what they did. For 3 years, the public soaked up these stories, and at least 15 men would be arrested and executed as a result of Oates' accusations. It was only when magistrates and the king himself began to grill Oates that authorities began to notice the holes and various inconsistencies in his stories. Eventually, Oates' house of cards came crashing down, and the gobsmacked public learned that no such plot had ever existed. The details of Oates' background check were published for the masses; Oates was a disgraced turncoat who had once belonged to the Catholic Church, but was expelled for "drunken blasphemy." Oates later became the chaplain for a royal navy ship, but he was once more dismissed for the crime of sodomy.

These stories had been nothing but the product of a vengeful madman's imagination. Years later, a judge declared many of these executed men posthumously innocent. This controversial event is now immortalized as the Popish Plot of 1678. While the muddied name of Titus Oates would never wash off, the damage had already been done. The largely Protestant public simply did not trust the Catholic Church.

Oates

The Popish Plot might have been purely fictitious, but things were about to get very real. In 1682, when the possibility of a Catholic king was soon to become a reality, anti-monarch extremists started to grow restless. The most devout partakers of the cause decided that something had to be done, and they began to conduct secret meetings to discuss their next move. Among these rebels were its leader, James Scott, the Duke of Monmouth and the illegitimate son of King Charles II; Lords Essex and William Russell; Sir Algernon Sydney; and Archibald Campbell, the Earl of Argyll. After the initial brainstorming session, the extremists had come to a consensus; the only way to ensure a future for Protestant England would be to kill the king and his proud Catholic brother, the Duke of York, then replace the monarch with James Scott, the Duke of Monmouth. One plotter suggested they shoot them from Bow Steeple, now known as the St. Mary-le-Bow Church. Another suggested that they make their move on Charles and James at St. James Park. Someone else proposed pouncing on the pair during a boat ride on the River Thames.

The Duke of Monmouth

Finally, a republican named Richard Rumbold cleared his throat, making himself heard. He offered his home, the Rye House, as their base, located just 18 miles outside of London. The well-to-do Civil War veteran lived in a handsome, fortified medieval mansion that was guarded by a moat. Eyes around the room brightened at once, and it was soon decided. Blueprints of the scheme were drawn. The attackers were to hide in the Rye House, where they would lie in wait. When an oblivious Charles and James returned from the horse races in Newmarket, the attackers would then leap out and lunge at them, slaying them on the spot. The plans were so detailed that nicknames were assigned to their targets. The sun-kissed Charles was named "Blackbird," and the fair-complexioned James was "Goldfinch."

The date of the assassination was planned for the 1st of April, 1683, but an unexpected turn of events would derail the entire mission. That afternoon, a major fire broke out in Newmarket, consuming half the city. The races were canceled, and the royal brothers returned to London early, completely unaware of how close they came to their deaths. 2 months later, a man named Josiah Keeling snitched on his conspirators, and the plot was made public. Over 2 dozen men were arrested for their involvement in the plot, and 12 would meet their grisly deaths – public executions where the men were hanged, drawn, and quartered. Another 2 were sentenced to death but would later be pardoned. At least 1 man suffered cruel and unusual punishment, and another committed suicide. 25 more were imprisoned, implicated, and fled into exile. Among the implicated was the Duke of Monmouth, but he would be pardoned and later moved to the Dutch Republic, where he lived for the time being. The nefarious failed scheme is now known as the "Rye House Plot."

By the 1680s, Catholicism had also begun to leave a bad taste in the mouths of the neighboring French people. In 1685, King Louis XIV rescinded the Edict of Nantes. The edict, which had been established by King Henry IV of France about a century prior, granted substantial rights and promoted religious tolerance to all men in the country, including the Calvinist Protestants. Louis, a known advocate for the Divine Right of Kings, declared Catholicism the dominant religion of France, and in doing so, he banned the practicing of all other religions, and set out on a mission to pluck the heretics out of the population. At the same time, he hounded the Protestants and forced them to convert with his policy of "dragonnades." Under this policy, special troops accosted and intimidated known Protestant families until they switched teams, or fled their homes.

In the months that followed, thousands of disheartened Protestants packed up their belongings and set out to search for greener pastures, so much so that by the early months of 1686, only an estimated 2,000 Protestants were left in France. Protestant defectors were soon scattered across Europe, and word about the wicked dangers of a Catholic tyranny had taken a life of its own. This was a fate that Protestants across the continent vowed to avoid at all costs.

On February 6, 1685, the 54-year-old King Charles II suffered a fatal apoplectic fit and passed away. With that, his younger brother James II was called upon to fill the vacant seat of the throne. The date of the coronation was set for 2 months later, on April 23rd, the Feast Day of St. George, England's patron saint.

And what a stupendous celebration it was. To commemorate the event, genealogist Francis Sandford was tasked with recording every last detail of the special day, from full descriptions of every scheduled event to intricate diagrams and drawings. The day kicked off with a procession from Westminster Hall to the Collegiate Church of St. Peter. Cheering crowds gathered in the streets to witness the momentous occasion, whistling and toasting their new king. A glowing James, along with the soon-to-be queen, Mary of Modena, waved at the sea of ruddy faces around them as trumpeters marched alongside them, the royals dressed in the finest robes made of purple velvet. The king's crown was breathtaking, crafted with velvet in a complementary shade of violet, studded with glittering diamonds and jewels, and topped off with a bedazzled crown ornament. The beautiful ceremony ended with a serenade from the heavenly voices of the choir, saluting the king with a Henry Purcell original, "My Heart is Inditing."

At 5:00 p.m., after a 5-hour long coronation ceremony, the new king and queen retired to Westminster Hall for a fabulous feast. The royals and their honored guests were seated around freshly polished tables boasting a jaw-dropping menu selection. The King and Queen themselves gorged on a total of 175 dishes, with 145 platters served as an appetizer course, and 30 dishes of hot meats in the following. A total of 1,445 dishes were served in the banquet hall that day, including "pistachio cream in glasses," "bolonia [sic] sausages," "pickled oysters," and "cold puffins." Every member of nobility had a servant hovering behind them, ready to cater to their every need. The celebratory fireworks, which were scheduled to be set alight over the picturesque view of the Thames River, was postponed to the following day.

As elaborately grand as the coronation was, the day seemed to be rife with bad omens. First, one of the canopy posts snapped, nearly crushing the king in the abbey. The crown, which had been exclusively minted for James II, did not fit him properly and nearly slipped off when it was placed on his head. The people whispered when the new king broke tradition by refusing the Anglican rite of communion, a featured event in all coronations before him.

The fireworks display was as impressive as it was disastrous, and a number of witnesses wrote about the catastrophe. Some of the rockets misfired, which prompted several boats to flip over in the chaos. What unfurled was a scene "so dreadful, that several spectators leaped into the river, choosing rather to be drowned than to be burned." At a nearby stable, spooked horses ran amok, leaving at least one coachman severely injured.

When James ascended to the throne in 1685, it appeared that he had hoped for a peaceful beginning. Bearing the sensitive religious tensions in his new country, James declared, "I shall make it my endeavor to preserve the government in Church and State as it is by law established. For a moment, Parliament and the Protestant public breathed easy.

One of James's first orders of business was to completely reconfigure the system. Top military and government officials were shuffled around and replaced with those known to be devout Catholics. Judges who did not concur with him were quickly booted out of the bench and substituted with justices who sided with his policies.

A brand new Parliament was set in place, each member a known James supporter. He created the Commission for Ecclesiastical Causes, devoted to punishing Anglican and Protestant clergymen who have either wronged him, or have refused to spread the Catholic word. Distinguished universities, including Christ Church and University College in Oxford, were now required by law to accept Catholic and other non-Protestant students. More eyes bulged when the king began to allow Catholics to hold important positions in university boards. The public was infuriated, but James was only warming up.

Shortly after James II rose to the throne, his reign was disrupted by 2 rebellions. The Duke of Monmouth had struck again, hungry for the crown. This time, Monmouth collaborated with another one of the alleged conspirators of the Rye House Plot, the Earl of Argyll. A third name is often associated as the great "plotter" of this new scheme: Robert Ferguson, a Scottish Presbyterian minister and the Duke's number one fan.

While in Holland, the duke and the earl had begun a public recruitment, assembling their army of riotous rebels, open to both men and women. The duke was able to attract a small, but feisty group of jaded farm workers, artisans, and other societal nonconformists, whereas the earl succeeded in collecting approximately 300 men for his campaign, known as the Campbells. Their new plan was set in motion – the earl was to take care of the royal forces based in Scotland, while the duke would deal with those in London. It must be noted that William of Orange was said to have been fully aware of the recruitment, but chose to turn a blind eye.

In early June, the earl and his Campbells crossed the seas to Scotland. There, the band quickly realized they had underestimated the size of the king's forces, and the mission was promptly cut short. On the 18th of that month, the earl was seized in the small Scottish village of Inchinnan. He was thrown into a prison in Edinburgh and was later sentenced to death. It was said that the smiling earl had taken his sentencing in stride. In fact, he had taken it so well, that he was found "sleeping soundly" by an official who had come expecting to drag him kicking and screaming to his death. He even bore these comforting words to his stepdaughter: "What shall I say in this great day of the Lord, wherein, in the midst of a cloud, I find a fair sunshine. I can wish no more for you...that the Lord may comfort you and shine upon you as he doth upon me, and give you that same sense of His love in staying in the world, as I have in going out of it."

Handling the Duke of Monmouth's forces was not as easy. The determined duke had pawned off many of his belongings for the occasion, using the funds to purchase ship, weaponry, and other necessary equipment for battle. His supportive wife and family pitched in with jewelry and other valuables of their own, providing him with extra funding. On the 11th of June, the duke proclaimed himself king in Lyme Regis, a charming coastal town in West England. Though the duke had only landed with just 1000 or so men, along with 3 small ships, 4 modest field guns, and just under 1,500 muskets, his band of rebels were less eager to surrender.

As luck would have it, James had been alerted of the duke's plans beforehand. The duke and his men were later easily defeated in the Battle of Sedgemoor. The duke was captured, taken to the Tower of London in mid-July, and had his head lopped off by the executioner, Jack Ketch. A thousand of these rebels were gathered and put on the hot seat in a series of trials known as the Bloody Assizes, which was overseen by 5 judges. 250 of these rebels were executed. One of the most controversial names among the sentenced was "gentlewoman" Dame Alice Lisle, who was found guilty and sent to burn at the stakes. As for the rest of the rebels, they were shipped off to the West Indies, where they were damned to live a life of "indentured servitude."

Perhaps as expected, James sought out to strengthen his defenses, amping up security for future rebellions that he knew was certain to come, and even after the early threats had petered out, he refused to dissolve his army. This immediately sent alarm bells ringing across the country. Doing so was strictly breaking code, as it was expected of rulers to disband armies during peacetime. Instead, James generated a "peacetime standing army" inspired by the French King Louis XIV.

Uniforms were introduced, weapons were upgraded, the required training now more extensive and hardcore, and a fixed rank system was set in place. 9 new infantry regiments (foot soldiers) and 7 cavalries (soldiers on horseback) were formed, and stationed all over England. A Catholic-run army was also raised in Ireland.

Naturally, this only worsened the already intense fear and rampant resentment against Catholics. Many raised a stink about it, fearing that the king would one day use this very army on his own subjects. More foreheads puckered when a few bad apples in the form of unruly soldiers began to stir up trouble and butt heads with the locals.

Apart from expanding the royal army, James disturbed the balance even more by adding a private council, consisting of all Catholic ministers. The Protestant public accused him of rubbing his Catholic faith in their faces. The king made no effort to conceal the Catholic masses held in the royal palace every week. It was against Parliament law for other religions to worship in public, but more Catholics began to step out of the dark, something the king encouraged heartily. James welcomed European Catholic missionaries into his land with open arms. Catholic chapels, schools, books, bibles, and other forms of media began to crop up all over England.

To the English Protestants, the most flagrant of these red flags were the king's continuous attempts to tackle traditional law. Week after week, James stood before Parliament, attempting to repeal the Test Acts, as well as all criminal laws that victimized Catholic and Protestant dissenters. When Parliament wagged their heads, rejecting his proposals, James ripped a page out of his brother's book and scrapped Parliament altogether.

James knew that he was treading on thin ice, and was quickly losing what few comrades he had. That same year, in 1686, the king met with the Quaker and founder of the Province of Pennsylvania, William Penn. A pact was formed between James, Penn, and other Protestant nonconformists, with all parties agreeing to provide support for one another to help ensure a future tolerant of all religions.

To the Protestants, the most problematic of the king's unremitting changes was the royal document he republished on April 4, 1688: The Declaration of Indulgence. The document aimed to negate all discriminatory laws on religion, and focused on 3 areas of change. First, all laws that penalized those of other religions who refused to attend or rejected communion rites from the Church of England were abolished. Second, people of all faiths were now allowed to worship in private houses or chapels. Third, the Test Acts would be canceled. No longer would those looking to advance in the government or military required to take various oaths outside of their preferred religion. These new laws applied to Protestants, Catholics, Jews, Muslims, Unitarians, and other nonconformists, including atheists. During a tour to promote this declaration of universal religious toleration, James stated, "...[S]uppose...there should be a law made that all black men should be imprisoned, it would be unreasonable and we had as little reason to quarrel with other men for being of different opinions as for being of different complexions."

The issuing of this declaration, on top of all of the king's other "adjustments," rattled the Anglican and Protestant clergymen. Their initial shock turned to bubbling bitterness when James ordered for these sacrilegious declarations to be read out from every pulpit in every church, or the "Order in Council." Blood pressures were spiking across the land.

To discuss the situation, the Archbishop of Canterbury, William Sancroft, invited 6 bishops to a private supper party in the borough of Lambeth in Central London. Grievances were laid out on the table, and solutions tossed around. By the time the last crumb had been licked from its plate, 7 of the clergymen signed a formal petition to denounce the Declaration of Indulgence. The petition claimed that the declaration was considered illegal under traditional Parliament law and should remain that way, as it threatened the fabric of Protestant English principles.

Sancroft

Sancroft himself had been the one to crown James, but now even he had come to his breaking point. The stark shift was staggeringly clear. On the 19th of May, the petition began to circulate in print, with anti-monarchists and rebels passing them out on the streets like last-day-sale flyers.

Out of the 100 or so churches in all of London, only 4 of these were said to have abided by the Order in Council.

One can only imagine how incensed the king must have been when word finally reached him. Almost at once, James slammed his foot down and had these bishops tried by a court of law under the charge of "seditious libel." During the trial, the bishops, under advice from their lawyers, kept a cool head. They would not admit to creating the petition, but would not withdraw from it, either. All throughout the trials, they calmly maintained that they had done nothing wrong. At every recess of their trials, they were greeted by hordes of supporters. Hundreds cheered the bishops on as they were being marched up and down the stairs of Whitehall. People, even nobles, waded through dirt and mud that reached their waists, all in the hopes of getting a quick blessing from the bishops. Many of these soldiers who were asked to guard the prisoners had also become enamored of them, and treated them with great respect. Eventually, the bishops were acquitted by the jury. The ecstatic crowds that gladly received them tripled in size.

Some of the bishops' supporters were the very nonconformists the king set out to free, but many saw the indulgence as a despicable act of bribery, aiming to destroy all the good that had been brought by the Reformation. One of James's loudest opponents was the dissenter and author of *Robinson Crusoe*, Daniel Defoe. A young Defoe was said to have declared, "I had rather the Church of England should pull our clothes off by fines and forfeitures, than the Papists should fall both upon the Church and the Dissenters, and pull our skins off by fire and faggott."

Defoe

Rumors, Conspiracy, and the Final Straw

"God be thanked we were not bred up in that communion but are of a Church that is pious and sincere, and conformable in all its principles to the Scriptures...the Church of England is, without all doubt, the only true Church." – Excerpt from a letter Princess Anne wrote to Mary, 1686

James's second wife, Mary of Modena, was as fertile as can be, but her children either perished in the womb or had their lives cut short by disease. Unwilling to give up, James and his wife tried just about every fertility treatment available at the time, even consuming wine mixed with hare spittle, floating bits of mice ears, bay-berries, eggs, and other roots and herbs. While these treatments might seem downright bizarre today, these practices were embraced by women and many medical experts of the time.

Something must have worked, because in fall of 1677, a delighted Mary of Modena announced that she was with child. In the early hours of June 10, 1688, a shrieking Mary doubled over in pain, feeling the blistering pains of labor contractions. Palace staff hastened to the royal bedchambers in clusters, watching anxiously by the door. As painful as it was, the labor only lasted a few hours, and by 10:00 a.m., the wailing baby had been born.

James and Mary were over the moon. After years and years of trial and error, they had finally produced a baby boy. They named him after the king, and from then on, the new prince was known as James Francis Edward. For weeks, doctors kept a close eye on the infant, feeding him postnatal gruel made of flour, water, sugar, and a splash of white wine, as well as milk from a wet nurse. James Francis was the picture of health – chubby, cherry-red cheeks, twinkling eyes, and a full head of thick, sandy-gold hair.

James Francis

The tidings of a healthy newborn are typically met with warm congratulations and jovial celebration, but with the introduction of James Francis, the Protestants were in uproar. As a matter of fact, James's very own children from his first marriage, Mary and Anne, wrinkled their noses at the news. Before James Francis, Mary and Anne had been the most likely candidates to succeed the throne, but this new male heir had set all their plans of reverting to a Protestant England ablaze. James Francis would undoubtedly be raised Catholic, thereby prolonging the dreaded Catholic rule.

This was when the rumors started pouring in, and James would see his own flesh and blood turn against him. Mary and Anne had never gotten along with their stepmother, Mary of Modena, who was only 4 years older than Mary, and with their new half-brother now on the scene, the sisters hatred for their stepmother only deepened. At the time, James's second daughter still resided in the palace, where she lived with her husband, Prince George of Denmark. Anne was the first to question the supposedly ill-fitting pieces to the puzzle, and began to question the circumstances surrounding the mysterious birth. For example, she wondered how Mary seemed to have recovered so quickly after childbirth, when during past births she would be bedridden for sometimes weeks at a time. Furthermore, she claimed that James had been far too confident about the gender of his child, almost as if he were certain of it, which was impossible in an age before ultrasounds. On top of that, some claimed that the baby boy had been smuggled into the queen's bed in a warming pan (an apparatus that resembles a frying pan with a lid on it; filled with coals and placed under beds). In other words, it was concluded that this boy was a "changeling."

Then came another rumor. Word on the street was that Mary of Modena had actually been adopted by the Duke of Modena, and that she was actually the secret daughter of Pope Clement X. Apparently, in 1673, young Mary had been convicted of a crime and was on the verge of being buried alive when Pope Clement came to her rescue. In exchange for her freedom, he instructed her to marry the Duke of York, securing their plan of Catholic domination in place.

Another tale was spun about the baby prince, who many mocked as the "Warming Pan Prince of Wales." Some suspected that his real father was Richard Talbot, Earl of Tyrconnell and Lord Lieutenant to James. His "real" mother is known only as an Irish woman named "Mrs. Gray." After the baby was taken from her, Mrs. Gray was shipped off to a secluded convent in Paris. She would later escape from the convent and attempt to locate her baby, only to be intercepted by Jesuits and promptly killed.

The propaganda against Prince James was stamped on thousands of pamphlets and hawked left and right. In spite of the documented 70 witnesses who were present during the birth, Princess Anne either firmly believed or chose to believe these tall tales. Mary, who was in the Netherlands, had also received word about the new addition to the family and began to exchange letters with her sister, sending long lists of questions and requesting regular updates. The sisters stroked their chins. Something just wasn't right.

Mary's husband would also begin to grow suspicious over his father-in-law's true motives. After all, he too, as James' son-in-law, was also in the running for the throne, something he believed that King Charles II, who had arranged his marriage with Mary, had intended. But whatever William suspected about the baby, he kept his opinions to himself.

Though James had initially opposed William and Mary's marriage, his relationship with his son-in-law enjoyed a promising start. During the Monmouth Rebellion, William had even sent Dutch mercenaries to England to help the struggling king.

Once James was crowned, however, their relationship began to strain. William began to grow suspicious of James, often questioning him about the king's ties to France. William reckoned that

James had forged a secret alliance with King Louis XIV, as James's military tactics and Catholic vision seemed greatly reminiscent of the French king. Even more suspicious, James would not return the favor when William asked for his help with his anti-French campaigns.

Whatever the case, the pair began to distance themselves from one another, and in January of 1688, James commanded William to remove all the English and Scottish armies based in the Netherlands. When William refused, a ruddy-faced James ordered all his men to simply desert William's forces and return to Britain. William, who did not want the extra weight of James's supporters dragging him down, swiftly agreed and bid them good riddance.

As another example, when James began his mission to repeal the Test Acts, he sought help from his son-in-law in Hague, but William would not bite, not even when William Penn was sent to the Hague on behalf of James. William opted to stay out of it, stating that he gave his full support to the Church of England. James would try again and again, assuring William that none of the rumors about his ties with the French were true. Still, William would not budge. He advised James to stick to the law and warned him that all these changes he was making would one day come back to haunt him. The equally stubborn James shrugged off William's many warnings.

William Penn

The Glorious Revolution

Historians believe it was Mary who first planted the idea of an English invasion in William's mind to depose James, which meant betraying her own father. But this was worth it to her because she believed the future of Protestant England was at stake.

Even so, an initially hesitant William would need a little more coaxing from his wife, because William's approval of the plan was supposedly hindered by his jealousy. He did not want to risk a second in the cold depths of her shadow; after all, if Mary was to take the throne, his wife, as the queen of England, would be more powerful than he was. It was only when an unyielding Mary convinced him that political power was the last thing on her mind that William began to shift his stance. Mary promised that she would stay by his side to the end as his wife, and "that she would do all that lay in her power to make him king for life." The pair finally agreed to an equal partnership, ruling as joint monarchs.

Some say that William had begun to plot for the invasion as early as November of 1687, when the news of Mary of Modena's pregnancy was first announced. Whether or not that is true is still up for debate, but what is known for certain is that by April of 1688, William had officially set his mind to the task. That month, William learned that King Louis and King James had signed off on a suspicious naval agreement that ensured France would provide funding for the English warships, which could only mean that James had been lying all along – the French and the English were, as he had always suspected, in cahoots.

With this in mind, the famously prudent William began to draw up plans for the invasion. He did not want to take on England without being certain that the people of England would have his back, because to do otherwise would be the move of an amateur. Indeed, the invasion would require some meticulous planning. Later that same month, William requested that a formal letter of invitation be sent to him by England's top-most politicians. A letter addressed to him by the "most valued men in the nation" showcasing their support would be the ultimate green light. If everything went as planned, he assured them that he would be ready by September.

Come May, William was greeted with bittersweet news. The rebels in England were growing antsy and did not want to wait any longer. They threatened to act now, with or without him. William was pleased to hear of their enthusiasm about putting an end to James's pro-Catholic reign, but he knew this was not the time. In fact, in early June, William sent an ambassador to James's palace to congratulate the king on his newborn son. This was allegedly just a front, because when William's agent left the palace, he secretly met with conspirators to smooth out the kinks of their plan and convinced them to hold on just a while longer to ensure a more triumphant outcome.

As rumors about Prince James Francis began to move throughout the kingdom, that letter William had been pining for arrived in the mail. He sliced off the wax seal excitedly, his heart thumping in his anticipation. His eyes settled on the signatures scrawled across the bottom of the letter – the Earl of Danby, the Earl of Shrewsbery, the Earl of Devonshire, Viscount Lumley, Admiral Edward Russell, Politician Henry Sydney, and Bishop Henry Compton – otherwise known as the "Immortal Seven." An excerpt from the letter read, "We have great reason to believe, we shall be everyday in a worse condition than we are, and less able to defend ourselves, and therefore we do earnestly wish we might be so happy as to find a remedy before it be too late for us to contribute to our own deliverance..."

Sydney

In hopes of restoring the power of the Church of England, as well as the creation of a new "free" Parliament, the Immortal Seven pledged their allegiance to William. The authors of the letter went on to declare that James had gone too far by abusing his "right of dispensation," playing puppeteer by overriding the laws of Parliament with his dreadful monarchy. The letter claimed that most officials in government were gravely discontent, and were only holding onto their jobs so that bills could be paid. The morale of the people was so low that "19 parts of 20 of the people throughout the country" all longed for change, and would give William their full support. William must have known that the statistic was a bit of an exaggeration, but nonetheless, their words were music to his ears.

In the first week of July, William Bentinck, one of William's most loyal associates, reached English soil, armed with satchels crammed with stacks of propaganda pamphlets. These pamphlets portrayed William as a knight in shining armor of sorts. The aspiring king was promoted as the best of all the Stuart candidates, and one who aimed to give the Protestant public (roughly 90% of the population) what they wanted. William swore he would ban the secret practicing of Catholicism and vowed to dismantle the tradition of absolutism, wherein the people were ruled under one monarch. He vowed to give more power to Parliament and the people. This same pamphlet also devoted a section to condemning the newborn, James Francis, who they branded the "Pretended [sic] Prince of Wales."

Thanks to Bentinck and his men, William secured most of the English public's support in less than 2 months. Even so, William was still leery of the alleged alliance between Louis and James, which would most certainly pose a problem for him in the future. More reinforcement was needed, so William sent another ambassador to the neighboring Austrian city of Vienna. His agent crept into the palace unnoticed, where he met with Holy Roman Emperor, Leopold I. A deal was struck up between both parties. William promised that by restoring Protestantism in England, he would not persecute the Catholics. If William kept up his end of the deal, Leopold would grant him a portion of his military when the time came. Lastly, Leopold agreed he would later join forces in an alliance against France.

Leopold I

The next step was to secure funding. Amsterdam was a global frontrunner in the 17th century, and the bustling financial hub of the world, making it a perfect bank of sorts. Be that as it may, actually acquiring a loan from the city would prove tougher than expected, as many of the top officials in the city were well-known supporters of the French. Thankfully for William, the French king would turn his Dutch supporters against him when he drove up tariffs and set limits on herring exports, which stung many Dutch businesses.

Eventually, 260 transports were hired. Bentinck, William's shining star, also began to drum up and negotiate contracts with mercenaries all over Europe, furthering the army expansion. By the end of Bentinck's endeavors, he had signed up over 13,500 German soldiers. The rest of William's loans came from unlikely sources. There was the Jewish banker, Francisco Suasso, who lent him a sum of 2 million guilders (approximately $200 million USD today). Suasso was supposedly so supportive that he did not ask for collateral. Taking a gamble, he told William to pay him back when he could, and if William failed to generate the funds, Suasso would simply take it as a loss. Another 4 million guilders were collected to patch up and bolster the fortresses in the east. Even Pope Innocent XI himself was said to have contributed to the funds, offering him a loan of at least 500,000 guilders. The Vatican would later deny that any such fund was provided for this purpose.

Bentinck

Suasso

Funds were also collected to pay the salaries of all the hired soldiers, along with 9,000 sailors. The ever fruitful Bentinck then traveled to the German city of Brandenburg to meet and sweet-talk the new elector. Another few thousand soldiers were added to William's disposal. By now, William and his men had amassed the following: 43 decked out and armed boats; 4 light frigates (another type of warship), and 10 "fireships" that could hold over 20,000 soldiers.

William may have garnered the support of almost all of England, but the same could not be said about his own people. No matter how hard he tried, he could not persuade his own top officials that this egregiously expensive expedition was absolutely necessary. Dutch officials were simply not swayed, and many of them feared going bankrupt. In response, one of the Immortal Seven suggested that they push the mission back a year, but William would not have it. The window of opportunity was quickly closing, and William feared they would never be able to squeeze through. At one point, these concerns had become so taxing that for a fleeting moment, William considered canceling the mission altogether.

Lo and behold, another window cracked open, and once again, it was the French king's own tempestuous temperament that made it happen. The pope refused to approve the candidate Louis had been heavily hyping for the Bishop of Cologne, which angered him so much that he decided to steer his attention towards Germany, springing to action before his French forces could be removed from the country. On September 9, 1688, the States General of the Netherlands was handed a pair of letters signed by King Louis. The first letter gruffly ordered the Dutch forces to keep away from England, and that they were not to, under any circumstances, disrupt the peace with English troops. In the second letter, the Dutch were asked not to pry their noses into the French movement in Germany. The startled Dutch general, along with his peers, were finally convinced that James was really working with the French after all. Later that week, Louis banished Dutch ships from all the ports in France.

Louis had allegedly done so to show the Dutch that he meant business, but this would blow up in his face. William reminded the Dutch officials of the horrors of 1672, when England and France had ganged up on the Netherlands. Hoping to avoid a repeat of history, the Dutch finally gave William their support on the 26th of September. James would continue to vehemently deny the allegiance, but this letter from Louis was all the proof they needed.

William's invasion fleet was a force of nature on its own. The Dutch army was at least 20,000 strong, though many of them were foreign mercenaries, including Scots, Swiss, Germans, and English rebels. A few dozen natives and 200 black men from Dutch-owned plantations in America were also brought on board. The troops were split into 3 squadrons of warships, which were to be led by Admirals Van Almonde, Herbert, and Eversten.

Meanwhile, massive container vessels were stuffed with 11,000 horses – including William's own personal coach and stallions – as well as over 20,000 rifles, ammunition, and other weapons. Other vessels contained a printing press, a portable bridge, a mobile blacksmith workshop, and molds for minting Orange-brand currency. A wide range of provisions were stocked, nourishment aplenty. There were 1,600 casks of beer and 50 more of brandy, each carrying 64 gallons of liquor, as well as 4 tons of tobacco and 10,000 pairs of boots to appease the troops.

On October 26, 1688, the Dutch warships, with William on the flagship, set sail for England. The Dutch spent the first few days coasting along the still waters, but before the second week's end, the fleet was ensnared in the eye of a sudden storm. While none of the men were hurt, they would lose about 1,300 horses. They suffocated behind their locked hatches, which had been sealed over with planks of wood as an emergency precaution.

Once the waters had calmed, the Dutch ships set sail once more. With the help of the so-called "Protestant Wind," an auspicious gust of wind from the east that blew west, the rest of the voyage carried on smoothly. As William's flagship, the Den Briel, sailed past the small Isle of Wight, the prince received his first boost of confidence. At least 300 of the island villagers had gathered by the shore, spurring them on with spirited whoops and hollers. The awe-stricken villagers marveled at the magnificent Dutch warships, the giant streamers tethered to the posts of the gleaming vessels rippling in the wind. Each streamer bore a different message. The one on William's ship bore the classic Orange motto, "Je Maintendrai." The others shared similar Latin slogans: "Pro libertate et religone." Together, the streamers proclaimed, "The Liberty of England and the Protestant Religion, I Will Maintain."

On the 15th of November (or the 5th of November in the Old Style Calendar), William and Mary finally reached solid ground. The fleet parked themselves at the coast of the small fishing town of Brixham, near the borough of Torbay. Upon landing, a Dutch chaplain who had come along summoned the troops for a prayer session. The soldiers linked hands and sang Psalm 118, an ode of gratitude to their God.

An equestrian portrait of William commemorating his landing

William's second confidence boost came from the villagers of Brixham, who were nothing but overjoyed to see the Dutch. The prince was instantly recognized by the distinctive coat of arms on the chest of his armor. Giddy villagers surrounded him, gushing their praises. Women stooped over to kiss his hands. A fisherman was said to have even swept William off his feet, prancing around with the prince on his shoulders. That evening, the villagers opened up their homes to William and his troops. They spoiled them with a feast and provided them with shelter for the night.

    3 days later, William and his army forged on to the cathedral city of Exeter, where he would meet even more of his fans. The prince was received with another round of celebrations as the congested streets, including local clergymen, toasted him and showered him with well wishes. There, the Dutch began their distribution of over 60,000 pamphlets, The Declaration of Hague. The pamphlets, which had been translated to English, reminded the people that William had arrived to free them from James' oppressive reign, along with other reiterations of his policies. The villagers would also be rewarded a glimpse of William's "fair ruling" when he had 2 of his own soldiers publicly executed after they were found guilty of swiping a chicken.

    In the days that followed, William was visited by powerful English officials, including the commander at the Plymouth Garrison, who offered William a healthy fraction of his troops. From there, William's army grew even stronger. His future was looking brighter than ever, and it was only now that James realized he was under attack. While James possessed a combined army of over 34,000 men, the majority of these soldiers were Protestants who would soon desert him. Before he could even summon his armies, the revolts had already begun, beginning with one in Cheshire County. He strove to stamp out William's forces, but he was met with one failure after another. Gradually, more and more of his generals began to abandon him to join William.

    The deflated English king was swiftly losing steam. The warm reception and hospitality his own people showed his son-in-law further disconcerted him. All the stress had also triggered a series of nosebleeds, which James considered yet another black omen. There was no denying it: the end seemed near.

    On the 7th of December, William and James' representatives convened at the Bear Inn in the town of Hungerford. William's smug agents slid a document across the table, which listed the prince's terms. The terms were: the dismissal of all Catholic officers, effective immediately; to retract all ill statements made against William and his party; for James to reimburse William for all the military costs of the expedition; and a promise from James that he would not seek help from French troops.

    William promoted a peaceful resolution to end all of the drama. He agreed to keep his army at bay, 40 miles west of London, if and only if James promised to do the same, but 40 miles to the east. In his terms, William showed no signs of his intentions to take over the throne. Instead, he appeared almost merciful and open to compromise with his father-in-law. James would be allowed to keep his crown, but his powers would considerably shrink.

    James received the terms the next evening, and assured William's agents that they would receive an answer the morning after. But the king had other plans. At this point, his wife, dressed as a laundrywoman, had already taken their child and escaped to France. James decided that he, too, would join them. On the night of December 11th, James set sail for France, accompanied by

2 Catholic comrades. As they sailed through the dark waters, James flung the "Great Seal of the Realm," the sovereign's official wax seal, over the side of the ship. Many saw this as a symbolic gesture of James's breakup with England.

James, a magnet for misfortune, would not go very far. Just 4 days later, he was apprehended by a pair of Kentish fishermen, towed back to English shore, and thrown into a cell. The disgraced king, who had now earned himself the unflattering nickname "Dismal Jimmy," would be locked behind bars for several days as the people called for his execution. In a final show of mercy, William allowed James to leave. And that he did. 2 days before Christmas, James left for England, never to return again.

With James gone, a unanimous decision was made by the House of Lords. They declared that King James had deserted his throne and was therefore stripped of his royal title. A week later, the crown was tendered to William and Mary, under the stipulation that Mary remain childless. At this juncture, Mary had been diagnosed with a critical illness and was now barren, so there was no need to think twice.

Though this stipulation was directed at Mary, it was no secret that William was in the driver's seat, and his wife, while sitting up front with him, was simply a passenger. The division of power was clear. The House of Lords would oversee civil administration, whereas William and Mary would have full control of the military. On the 29th of December, the pair were put in charge of the temporary government.

For Mary, this victory had come with a price. A part of her was conflicted for having betrayed her own father, but at the end of the day, there had been no other alternative. Freedom from James's incompetence and disorderly reign, Mary believed, was for the good of the people. It was what they needed and what they deserved.

In February of 1689, Mary finally reunited with her husband in Greenwich. That month, Parliament, along with the Tories and the Whigs, gathered to create the "Declaration of Rights." This document would later be amended and given a new title – the "Bill of Rights." The bill listed in detail the terms and regulations the monarchs-to-be were to abide by if they were to be given the crown. First and foremost, Parliament was to schedule regular meetings more frequently. The Parliament would essentially hold more power. The monarchs were not allowed to interfere with the selection of Parliament members, but possessed the right to veto bills and may pardon whoever they choose to. The monarchs were not permitted a standing army or embark on any military campaigns without Parliament's consent.

The bill would also protect the English people. Freedom of speech would be guaranteed to all. Unhappy citizens, no matter what creed, were free to petition for whatever cause they pleased. A Toleration Act was later passed so that no more would be compelled to join the Church of England. That said, Protestant nonconformists and other dissenters were still made to shell out a tenth of their annual earnings to the Church of England, which were taxes known as "tithes."

Moreover, the monarchs would no longer hold the right to determine the religion of his or her subjects, as religion was now separate from politics. Kings and queens must now accept that they were second to Parliament in power, and the policy of the "Divine Right of Kings" was officially extinct. England was now a true constitutional monarchy. This new government formed the foundations of the modern British Parliament.

Britain's first and only coronation for joint sovereigns was set for April 11, 1689. This was William and Mary's special day, and the exuberance that had overcome the public was infectious, but clearly not everyone was in the mood for celebrating. That morning, Mary received a strongly-worded letter from James. He reproached her, "The curses of an angry father will fall on you, as well as those of a God who commands obedience to his parents." With a heavy heart, Mary crumpled up the letter and chucked it aside, determined not to let anything put a damper on her day. William and Mary appeared at Westminster Abbey, where the Declaration of Rights was read to them once more. Once the pair had agreed, they were crowned by Henry Compton, the Bishop of London.

After a 3-hour ceremony, the new monarchs emerged from behind the glossy timber doors. The couple strode down the stairs, their ceremonial robes swishing majestically around their feet. Sporting a lustrous bejeweled crown with a velvet bonnet, King William waved at the whistling congregation in front of him. Next to him stood Queen Mary in a twinkling tiara, with her beaming face immaculately painted, radiating pride. The husband and wife would later enjoy a lovely banquet, with festivities lasting until 10 in the evening.

The striking saga of the Glorious Revolution is one that continues to fascinate historians around the world today. Some chroniclers have referred to these events as the "Bloodless Revolution," but other historians say otherwise. The ruthless game of politics that William and James played may have been somewhat bloodless in comparison to history's greatest rebellions, but the rebels, soldiers, and other pawns who lost their lives along the way must not be forgotten. The revolution would also pave the path for a series of bloody wars between England and Scotland, the result of which has left quite a legacy of its own.

Online Resources

Other books about English history by Charles River Editors

Other books about the Glorious Revolution on Amazon

Bibliography

1. Vallance, Edward, PhD. "The Glorious Revolution." BBC . BBC, 17 Feb. 2011. Web. 16 Jan. 2017.
<http://www.bbc.co.uk/history/british/civil_war_revolution/glorious_revolution_01.shtml>.

2. Handlin, Emily. "The History of the Coronation of James II." Brown University Library. History of Art and Architecture Department, 2012. Web. 16 Jan. 2017.
<http://library.brown.edu/readingritual/handlin_jamesII.html>.

3. Knowles, Rachel. "The Whigs and the Tories." Regency History. Blogger, 21 Apr. 2015. Web. 16 Jan. 2017. <http://www.regencyhistory.net/2015/04/the-whigs-and-tories.html>.

4. Trueman, C. N. "The 1688 Revolution." The History Learning Site. The History Learning Site, Ltd., 16 Aug. 2016. Web. 16 Jan. 2017. <http://www.historylearningsite.co.uk/stuart-england/the-1688-revolution/>.

5. Trueman, C. N. "The Popish Plot." The History Learning Site. The History Learning Site, Ltd., 17 Mar. 2015. Web. 16 Jan. 2017. <http://www.historylearningsite.co.uk/stuart-england/the-popish-plot/>.

6. Rennell, Tony. "The 1688 invasion of Britain that's been erased from history." The Daily Mail. Associated Newspapers, Ltd., 18 Apr. 2008. Web. 16 Jan. 2017. <http://www.dailymail.co.uk/news/article-560614/The-1688-invasion-Britain-thats-erased-history.html>.

7. Stocker, Barry. "The Glorious Revolution and the Immortal 7's Letter." Bosphorus Reflections: Barry Stocker's Weblog. Blogger, 2 July 2009. Web. 16 Jan. 2017. <http://www.bbc.co.uk/history/people/william_iii_of_orange>.

8. Jonathan. "Great Events in British History: William of Orange and the Glorious Revolution." Anglotopia. Anglotopia, LLC, 8 June 2015. Web. 16 Jan. 2017. <http://www.anglotopia.net/british-history/great-events-in-british-history-william-of-orange-and-the-glorious-revolution/>.

9. Editors, Britannia. "William III and Mary II (1689-1702 AD)." Britannia. Britannia, LLC, 2012. Web. 16 Jan. 2017. <http://www.britannia.com/history/monarchs/mon51.html>.

10. Heathcoate, John. "Pope cut out of Orange history." FantomPowa. N.p., 1998. Web. 16 Jan. 2017. <http://www.fantompowa.net/Flame/pope_cut_out_of_.htm>.

11. Editors, CRF. "England's Glorious Revolution." Constitutional Rights Foundation. Constitutional Rights Foundation, 2017. Web. 16 Jan. 2017. <http://www.crf-usa.org/bill-of-rights-in-action/bria-25-3-england-glorious-revolution.html>.

12. Editors, SMLOL. "The Glorious Revolution of 1688." THE SOMME MEMORIAL LOYAL ORANGE LODGE 842. THE SOMME MEMORIAL LOYAL ORANGE LODGE, 2009. Web. 16 Jan. 2017. <http://www.lol842bristol.com/index.php?p=1_36_Glorious-Revolution>.

13. Admin, HIH. "England and the Popish Plot." History in an Hour. WordPress, 17 Oct. 2010. Web. 16 Jan. 2017. <http://www.historyinanhour.com/2010/10/17/england-and-the-popish-plot/>.

14. Petty, Mike. "The Classic Sir Edmund Berry Godfrey Coincidence Which Isn't Quite What It Appears." 67 Not Out. Blogger, 16 Aug. 2013. Web. 16 Jan. 2017. <http://www.67notout.com/2013/08/the-classic-sir-edmund-berry-godfrey.html>.

15. Editors, History Channel. "Enlightenment." History Channel. A&E Television Networks, LLC, 2016. Web. 16 Jan. 2017. <http://www.history.com/topics/enlightenment>.

16. Editors, SparkNotes. "THE ENLIGHTENMENT (1650–1800)." SparkNotes. SparkNotes, LLC, 2015. Web. 16 Jan. 2017. <http://www.sparknotes.com/history/european/enlightenment/terms.html>.

17. Editors, Kepler College. "Francis Bacon: The Natural Philosopher." Kepler College. Kepler College, 2015. Web. 16 Jan. 2017. <http://www.kepler.edu/home/index.php/articles/history-of-astrology/item/333-francis-bacon-the-natural-philosopher>.

18. Editors, Biography Online. "John Locke biography." Biography Online. Biography Online, 2014. Web. 16 Jan. 2017. <http://www.biographyonline.net/writers/john-locke-biography.html>.

19. Brom, Robert H. "Papal Infallibility." Catholic Answers. Catholic Answers, 10 Aug. 2004. Web. 16 Jan. 2017. <https://www.catholic.com/tract/papal-infallibility>.

20. Morris, Marc. "King John: the most evil monarch in Britain's history." The Telegraph. Telegraph Media Group, Ltd., 13 June 2015. Web. 16 Jan. 2017. <http://www.telegraph.co.uk/culture/11671441/King-John-the-most-evil-monarch-in-Britains-history.html>.

21. Nix, Elizabeth. "8 Things You Might Not Know about Mary I." History Channel. A&E Television Networks, LLC, 16 Feb. 2016. Web. 16 Jan. 2017. <http://www.history.com/news/8-things-you-might-not-know-about-mary-i>.

22. Trueman, C. N. "Louis XIV and religion." The History Learning Site. The History Learning Site, Ltd., 17 Mar. 2015. Web. 16 Jan. 2017. <http://www.historylearningsite.co.uk/france-in-the-seventeenth-century/louis-xiv-and-religion/>.

23. Editors, History Channel. "Great Fire of London begins." History Channel. A&E Television Networks, LLC, 2 Sept. 2015. Web. 16 Jan. 2017. <http://www.history.com/this-day-in-history/great-fire-of-london-begins>.

24. Shimmin, Graeme. "Are there any conspiracy theories behind the Great Fire of London?" Quora. Quora, Inc., 19 Dec. 2013. Web. 16 Jan. 2017. <https://www.quora.com/Are-there-any-conspiracy-theories-behind-the-Great-Fire-of-London>.

25. McRobbie, Linda Rodriguez. "The Great Fire of London Was Blamed on Religious Terrorism." The Smithsonian Magazine. The Smithsonian Institution, 2 Sept. 2016. Web. 17 Jan. 2017. <http://www.smithsonianmag.com/history/great-fire-london-was-blamed-religious-terrorism-180960332/>.

26. Porter, Margaret. "A Coronation Feast, 23 April, 1685." English Historical Fiction Authors. Blogspot, 23 Feb. 2015. Web. 17 Jan. 2017. <http://englishhistoryauthors.blogspot.tw/2015/02/a-coronation-feast-23-april-1685.html>.

27. Editors, Encyclopedia.Com. "James II (King Of England, Scotland, And Ireland)." Encyclopedia.Com. The Columbia University Press, 2014. Web. 17 Jan. 2017. <http://www.encyclopedia.com/people/history/british-and-irish-history-biographies/james-ii-england>.

28. Editors, History Channel. "King Charles I executed for treason." History Channel. A&E Television Networks, LLC, 30 Jan. 2015. Web. 17 Jan. 2017. <http://www.history.com/this-day-in-history/king-charles-i-executed-for-treason>.

29. Editors, Scandalous Women. "Royal Mistresses: Catherine Sedley, Countess of Dorchester." Scandalous Women. Blogspot, 27 Aug. 2008. Web. 17 Jan. 2017. <http://scandalouswoman.blogspot.tw/2008/08/royal-mistresses-catherine-sedley.html>.

30. Derrick, Kiri. "Top 10 Philandering English Monarchs." Listverse. Listverse, Ltd., 21 Apr. 2011. Web. 17 Jan. 2017. <http://listverse.com/2011/04/21/top-10-philandering-english-monarchs/>.

31. Editors, Parliament UK. "Whigs and Tories." Parliament UK. Parliament UK, 2015. Web. 17 Jan. 2017. <http://www.parliament.uk/about/living-heritage/evolutionofparliament/parliamentaryauthority/revolution/overview/whigstories/>.

32. Editors, Parliament UK. "Catholics and Protestants." Parliament UK. Parliament UK, 2015. Web. 17 Jan. 2017. <http://www.parliament.uk/about/living-heritage/evolutionofparliament/parliamentaryauthority/revolution/overview/catholicsprotestants/>.

33. Editors, Your Dictionary. "William III Facts." Your Dictionary. Love To Know Corporation, 2013. Web. 17 Jan. 2017. <http://biography.yourdictionary.com/william-iii>.

34. Editors, Encyclopedia.Com. "Mary II." Encyclopedia.Com. The Gale Group, Inc., 2015. Web. 17 Jan. 2017. <http://www.encyclopedia.com/people/history/british-and-irish-history-biographies/mary-ii>.

35. Editors, English Monarch. "William III and Mary II." English Monarchs. English Monarchs, 2005. Web. 17 Jan. 2017. <http://www.englishmonarchs.co.uk/stuart_6.htm>.

36. Lucy, Gordon. "Share: The Legacy Of William Of Orange." The Orange Order. Grand Orange Lodge of Ireland, 2012. Web. 17 Jan. 2017. <http://www.grandorangelodge.co.uk/history.aspx?id=99484#.WIGpH_l95EZ>.

37. Dennison, Matthew. "The merry monarch and his mistresses; was sex for Charles II a dangerous distraction?" The Spectator. The Spectator, Ltd., 31 Jan. 2015. Web. 17 Jan. 2017.

<http://www.spectator.co.uk/2015/01/the-merry-monarch-and-his-mistresses-was-sex-for-charles-ii-a-dangerous-distraction/>.

38. "First Inaugural Address of Abraham Lincoln." The Avalon Project. Lillian Goldman Law Library, 2008. Web. 17 Jan. 2017. <http://avalon.law.yale.edu/19th_century/lincoln1.asp>.

39. Editors, The Reformation. "The Rye House Plot 1683." The Reformation. WordPress, 12 Mar. 2016. Web. 17 Jan. 2017. <http://www.thereformation.info/rye_house_plot.htm>.

40. Editors, GMMG. "THE LAST SLEEP OF THE EARL OF ARGYLL." Greater Manchester Museum Group. Greater Manchester Museum Group, 2013. Web. 17 Jan. 2017. <http://www.gmmg.org.uk/our-connected-history/item/last-sleep-of-argyll/>.

41. Editors, HH. "Dame Alice Lisle." Hampshire History. Hampshire History, 28 Oct. 2013. Web. 18 Jan. 2017. <http://www.hampshire-history.com/dame-alice-lisle/>.

42. Editors, New World Encyclopedia. "James II of England." New World Encylopedia. MediaWiki, 27 Apr. 2014. Web. 18 Jan. 2017. <http://www.newworldencyclopedia.org/entry/James_II_of_England>.

43. Campbell, K. K. "King Louis XIV: French Mastermind." History Net. World History Group, 12 June 2006. Web. 18 Jan. 2017. <http://www.historynet.com/king-louis-xiv-french-mastermind.htm>.

44. Editors, Spanish Succession. "The English Army." Spanish Succession. N.p., 2015. Web. 18 Jan. 2017. <http://www.spanishsuccession.nl/english_army.html#3>.

45. McFerran, Noel S. "Declaration of Indulgence of King James II, April 4, 1687." The Jacobite Heritage. Noel McFerran, 25 Oct. 2003. Web. 18 Jan. 2017. <http://www.jacobite.ca/documents/16870404.htm>.

46. Scrivener, Patrick. "THE WARMING PAN PRINCE OF WALES PLOT EXPOSED AT LAST!!" Reformation.Org. Patrick Scrivener, 2016. Web. 18 Jan. 2017. <http://www.reformation.org/warming-pan-prince-of-wales-plot-exposed.html>.

47. Taylor, Jerome. "When 17th-century women would seek out hare spittle." The Independent. Associated Newspapers, Ltd., 29 Nov. 2007. Web. 18 Jan. 2017. <http://www.independent.co.uk/life-style/health-and-families/features/when-17th-century-women-would-seek-out-hare-spittle-760836.html>.

48. Smitha, Frank E. "William and Mary, a Glorious Revolution and Bill of Rights." Macro History and World Timeline. Frank E Smitha, 2015. Web. 18 Jan. 2017. <http://www.fsmitha.com/h3/h25eng5.htm>.

49. Childs, John. Army, James II and the Glorious Revolution. N.p.: Manchester U Press, 1980. Print.

50. Craik, George Lillie. The Pictorial History of England During the Reign of George the Third. Vol. 3. N.p.: RareClub.com, 2012. Print.

51. Aubrey, John. Aubrey's Brief Lives. N.p.: Nonpareil , 2015. Print.

52. Instructor, The Catholic. The Catholic Instructor. Vol. 3. N.p.: RareClub.com, 2012. Print.

53. Alexander, Rachel. Myths, Symbols and Legends of Solar System Bodies (The Patrick Moore Practical Astronomy Series). N.p.: Springer, 2015. Print.

54. Crompton, Louis. Homosexuality and Civilization. N.p.: Belknap Press, 2006. Print.

55. Starkey, David. "The Glorious Revolution." Monarchy with David Starkey. Dir. James Burge. BBC. 20 Nov. 2006. Television.

Free Books by Charles River Editors

We have brand new titles available for free most days of the week. To see which of our titles are currently free, click on this link.

Discounted Books by Charles River Editors

We have titles at a discount price of just 99 cents everyday. To see which of our titles are currently 99 cents, click on this link.

Printed in Great Britain
by Amazon